Brother Max:
Labour Organizer and Educator

Brother Max:
Labour Organizer and Educator

Max Swerdlow

Edited by Gregory S. Kealey
St. John's: Committee on Canadian Labour History

Committee on Canadian Labour History
Department of History
Memorial University of Newfoundland
St. John's, Newfoundland
A1C 5S7
Canada

ISBN 0-9692060-8-9

Keyboarded and typeset by the Committee on Canadian Labour History

Printed and bound in Canada
Printed by Robinson-Blackmore Printing & Publishing Limited

Cover photos: Front: *May Day 1969 Georgetown, Guyana. Richard Ishmael, President of the Guyana Trade Union Council with Max and Anne Swerdlow;* Back: *May Day 1969.*

Canadian Cataloguing in Publication Data

Swerdlow, Max, 1915-1990

Brother Max: Labour Organizer and Educator

ISBN 0-9692060-8-9

1. Swerdlow, Max, 1915-1990. 2. Trade-unions — Canada — Officials and employees — Biography. I. Committee on Canadian Labour History.
II. Title.

HD6525.S83A3 1990   331.88'092   C90-097647-0

To my wife, Anne
who was fully involved in my work and
whose boundless help and wise counsel
added significantly to the substance and
excitement of our lives.

You can't organize successfully without educating;
you can't educate effectively without organizing.

Max Swerdlow

Max Swerdlow died on 21 October 1990 while this book was in press.
The Committee on Canadian Labour History also dedicates it to his memory.

TABLE OF CONTENTS

ABBREVIATIONS

AFL — American Federation of Labor

AFL-CIO — American Federation of Labor and Congress of Industrial Organization

CAAE — Canadian Association for Adult Education

CBRE — Canadian Brotherhood of Railway Employees

CCCL — Canadian and Catholic Confederation of Labour

CCL — Canadian Congress of Labour

CCF — Cooperative Commonwealth Federation

CIO — Congress of Industrial Organization

CLC — Canadian Labour Congress

CNTU — Confederation of National Trade Unions

ICFTU — International Confederation of Free Trade Unions

ILGWU — International Ladies' Garment Workers' Union

ILO — International Labour Organization

NDP — New Democratic Party

TLC — Trades and Labour Congress of Canada

UAW — United Automobile Workers

FOREWORD

MAX SWERDLOW was a remarkable Canadian. I first knew him as a Director of the Frontier College, where I worked as a labourer-teacher in the early 1960s. By this time, Brother Max was the most experienced labour educator in Canada. On Frontier's Board he represented the Canadian Labour Congress and was instrumental in cementing a working relationship with corporate leaders towards a common interest — promoting human development in outlying communities throughout the country. His influence at the Frontier College was so strong that his presence remained powerful long after his departure to international assignments later that decade.

It would be difficult today to estimate how many labour educators are at work in Canada. Yet, only a few decades ago, they were small in number and Max Swerdlow was their mentor. In his words, "since none of us was a trained labour educator, we relied on each other for ideas, advice and assistance. Our inter-dependence resulted in a close knit group of colleagues and good friends." He blazed a trail and set high standards.

When I first saw the manuscript for this book, Max told me that he has often been asked "What does a labour educator do?" *Brother Max: Labour Organizer and Educator* was his answer. His purpose in writing was to illuminate and share his life's work in labour education. While this volume is not intended as labour history, or autobiography, or a text book, it contains elements of all three. Readers will find it at once entertaining, enlightening and inspiring. Through Max's eyes, we also gain insights into the work of others, leaders such as Claude Jodoin, Howard Conquergood, Gower Markle and Roby Kidd.

I do not know which of his many achievements gave Max Swerdlow the greatest satisfaction. But what a list of candidates! Leadership of the CLC's Education Department. Establishing the Labour College of Canada. Animation on behalf of the International Labour Organization in the Caribbean and in Asia. Establishing the principle that making love in a storeroom is not a cause for dismissal under a collective agreement.

I invite readers to join with me in celebrating the life and work of a great Canadian. Through his example, well documented here, he inspired a new generation to excel in a noble goal — creating a humane, just, and democratic society; a learning society led by learning adults.

Ian Morrison
Executive Director
Canadian Association for Adult Education

PHOTOGRAPHS

1. TLC Policy and Negotiating Committee, DIL Industries, Valleyfield, Quebec, 1943-1944.

2. TLC Quebec Organizer. Front row from left: Emile Nantel, unknown, Rosaire Desjardins, Jean LaRiviere; Back row: Phil Cutler, Bernard Boulanger, Neil McDonald, unknown, Max Swerdlow.

3. Bargaining Committee, DIL, Valleyfield, 1943. In centre of photo is Robert Haddow.

4. Cartoon depicting TLC/CCL Merger Talks. From *The Third Page*, Windsor, 2 June 1955.

5. 35th Session of the ILO, Geneva, 1952. Left to right: Paul Goulet, Director, ILO; M.M. Maclean, Assistant Deputy Minister of Labour; Leon Jauhaux, President, Force ouvriere, France; Max Swerdlow.

6. TLC-CCL Joint Policy Conference, Kitchener, Ontario, 1953.

7. TLC Organization and Education Field Staff, 1956.

8. Canadian Conference on Education, Ottawa, 1958. Left to right: Lt. Col. K.R. Swinton, Dr. Wilder G. Penfield, Max Swerdlow.

9. ICFTU-ILO, Seminar on Labour Participation in Economic Development, Singapore, 1974.

10. ILO, Trade Union Seminar on Population Questions, Calcutta, 1973.

11. Breaking ground for the Critchlow Labour College, Georgetown, Guyana, 1968. From left to right: Richard Ishmael (with spade), Prime Minister Forbes Burnam, Max Swerdlow.

12. Architect's Model, Critchlow Labour College. Left to right: Richard Ishmael, Prime Minister Forbes Burnam, Architect George Henry, Max Swerdlow, Claude Marriman, Minister of Labor.

CHAPTER ONE
Riding the Freight

THE TRAIN WAS OUT OF REGINA, bound for Montreal, and I had a box car all to myself. It was not the first time I had travelled this way; but this time it was different. It was the end of April 1934, May Day was near and, since I was about 15, I had always taken part in celebrations of that international labour holiday.

Now, at the age of 19, I was lonely and felt somewhat guilty. I thought back to the May Day rallies I had attended in Winnipeg, Regina, and other centres. I missed the fiery speeches and the cheers of the crowds. The rallies had, for me, been a source of inner strength, challenge, and defiance. These were the Hungry Thirties, and I was one of thousands who were aimlessly "riding the rods," "sleeping in jungles," and walking the streets in search of work and food, or just chasing rainbows.

But I had stars in my eyes and I refused to accept the deprived and meaningless life of so many around me. I was aware of the injustices of the social system, and I blamed capitalism — the greed of the rich and the indifference and callousness of politicians. I was a rebel, but a rebel with a cause.

As the train rolled along, images of the past unfolded with all their excitements, difficulties, and adventures. This was what had shaped, and would continue to shape, the tapestry of my life.

I was born in Odessa, Russia, in 1915, at a time when my family was caught in the turmoil and disorder between the outbreak of World War I in 1914 and the Bolshevik Revolution of 1917. Before the war my grandmother, uncles, and aunt had emigrated to the United States. My parents and grandfather were to follow; but when the war broke out, immigration into the United States was restricted, and they were unable to leave.

Both my parents were performers in the Jewish theatre, and my father was particularly talented. When I was about two, and my brother one, my father was drafted into the Russian army and sent to the Austrian front, where he was taken prisoner and held until the end of hostilities in 1918. He then returned to Odessa and resumed his efforts to get our family to America. My grandfather had decided to remain in Russia.

Finally, in the summer of 1923, we left Odessa for Bremen, Germany, from where we were to sail to the United States. At Bremen we were taken to a quarantine compound on the outskirts of the city. Surrounded by a high stone wall, the compound comprised several dormitories, each housing about 75 men, women, and children. They slept in double-decked bunks and ate from long uncovered tables in a common room that also served as a recreation hall. We soon learned there were hundreds like us, waiting their turn to sail.

Soon after we arrived we were told that only my father could be admitted to the United States. He qualified since most of his family was already there. My mother, brothers, and I would have to wait until immigration regulations were eased. My parents were deeply depressed. The question was whether my father should go on alone, or wait with us; for how long we did not know. They agonized over this for several days and finally decided he should go. The rest of us began to adjust to a monotonous, uneventful but reasonably secure life in "The Quarantine."

Shortly after my father arrived in the United States he was engaged by the Jewish Art Theatre in New York. He wrote us regularly, but was unable to tell us when we might join him. In one of his letters he said he was going on a tour of several American and Canadian cities. It was several months before we heard from him again, and then the letter came from Canada. He wrote that after an engagement in Winnipeg he had run into complications with the United States immigration authorities and had been refused readmission. As a result he had decided to remain in Winnipeg as a landed immigrant, and, at the same time, he had applied for permission to bring us to Canada.

This was one more disturbing surprise. We had heard a great deal about the promised land of the United States, but Canada was completely unknown to us. We thought it might be months, or even years, before we were permitted to enter this strange country, and we slowly became resigned to an unpredictable future.

In 1923 I celebrated my eighth birthday, and my mother arranged for me to attend a public school in Bremen. This was a new experience, and I liked it. I made friends with some German children and quickly learned to speak their language, in addition to the Russian and Yiddish I already knew. I vividly remember the teacher, Herr Schwartz. He was a man of about 30 years, always well groomed and immaculately dressed. He spoke in short, crisp, and precise sentences, but not in a commanding manner.

He was serious and business-like, even with children of our age. A strict disciplinarian, he expected his students to be alert and to refrain from unnecessary conversation. He often held a long bamboo stick, which he threatened to use on anyone who misbehaved, though he never did. He would, however, slam it on the desk in front of an offending student, and the deafening sound frightened the whole class into deadly silence, at least for a time. His worst punishment was to seize the offender's sideburn and pull it, often lifting the student with it.

The periods I found most interesting were those in which he read to us — the epic tales of Siegfried, Karl May's stories of North American Indians, and Edgar Rice Burroughs' adventures of Tarzan were the best. I liked going to school, particularly because it provided an opportunity to escape from the confines of "The Quarantine."

Finally, in late 1925, we received the welcome news that our application had been accepted and we should be ready to sail for Canada on short notice. We left Bremen just before Christmas and arrived at Halifax 3 January 1926. From there we went by train to Winnipeg, where we joined my father and settled. We had become Canadians, almost by accident.

My brother and I were quickly enrolled in a school where we made rapid progress in English, just as quickly forgetting the Russian and German languages. At first I did well at school, even skipping some grades, but by the time I reached Grade Eight, the highest of my formal education, I was, at thirteen, the oldest in the class.

For about two years I studied the violin with an acquaintance of the family, and then my father arranged for me to study under John Waterhouse, the founder and conductor of the Winnipeg String Orchestra, and the most prominent music teacher in the city. After about a year he asked me if I would like to play in the second violin section of his orchestra. It was a great honour, and of course I accepted. For several weeks I studied the music that was to be on the programme, and my parents were proud that their son should play in such a large orchestra. It was, however, not only my first, but also my last appearance.

After school hours I attended a Jewish parochial school. My parents wanted me to study Jewish literature and culture, and, above all, not to forget the Jewish language. At the Workmen's Circle School, an offshoot of the socialist movement in Europe, I studied both classical and contemporary Jewish literature, and was introduced to several political "isms" including Marxism, Leninism, Trotskyism, anarchism and others. I suspect these were subjects that my father did not anticipate I would study.

It was traditional among Jewish families that when their eldest son reached the age of 13, his bar mitzvah, marking his arrival at manhood, should be the cause of a celebration. And so, some months before my thirteenth birthday, my parents began making plans. I stopped going to the Workmen's Circle School and began new studies in a Chader, or Rabbinical School. There I was instructed in the Jewish religion, the Hebrew language, and undertook the preparation of a speech in Hebrew to be delivered at my bar mitzvah. Every morning, before going to school, I attended service in the synagogue.

My bar mitzvah took place 1 March 1928, with my parents and friends gathering at the synagogue to participate in my initiation into manhood. I wore a new three-piece suit, had my own prayer shawl, and carried the small box containing Hebrew texts, known as phylactery. The ceremony went off smoothly and my Hebrew speech was well received. The festivities that followed were brief and modest. Most of the guests had a drink of whiskey or wine and a piece of cake. They shook hands with me and my father and then left.

As of that day I was no longer a boy; I was a man, a mature adult. Yet I did not feel different. It seemed that I had been an adult for a long time. Much had contributed to making me a rather serious young man: the trauma of hunger in Russia, the anxiety of life in the Bremen Quarantine, the separation of our family, the dramatic change of life in the new world, learning new languages, and the theatrical life-style of my parents, which I disliked.

The days immediately following my bar mitzvah were uneventful. I stopped going to the Hebrew School, but went to the Workmen's Circle and the public school, as well as continuing my musical studies. Then, in 1929, the Great Depression began to unfold. The Jewish Theatre in Winnipeg closed, and my parents were unemployed. My father found part-time work painting houses. I left school and gave up music to be his helper; but the two of us could not earn enough to support the family and we went on relief. The weekly parcel of food we received, with the little we earned painting, provided for the family's basic needs. But after a few months the painting contractor told us there was no more work, and we were once again all unemployed. My father had no skill, apart from acting, nor could he easily learn another trade. Nevertheless, a tailor friend offered to teach him tailoring. He was to work for a month without pay, and then he would be on a piece-work rate, paid according to his production. He accepted the offer.

By 1930 the Depression had become devastating. At 15 I was neither in school nor at work. One day as I walked aimlessly past the Market Square, behind the Winnipeg City Hall, I saw a crowd gathered around a truck from which a man was speaking, emphasizing his points by vigorously waving his arms. This was one of the almost daily rallies of the unemployed. I joined the crowd and listened to one speaker after another. I was impressed. They were accusing, demanding, defying, and challenging the government and authorities. They argued that the appalling conditions to which the unemployed were subject were inherent to the capitalist system, which had to be wiped out. They pleaded for unity among workers to join in this militant struggle.

All of this seemed to me to make sense, and I attended more and more rallies, soon getting to know some of the activists in the unemployed movement. One day I was asked if I would help in handing out circulars on the street, and I readily agreed. I went to the Workers' Centre, which was in an old converted church building. There I was given a supply of circulars and set out with an older fellow. As we handed out the leaflets, we occasionally engaged in conversation about the unemployed movement or the discredited capitalist system. I liked the experience and frequently went to the Centre and took part in leafleting.

Then one of the leaders asked me if I would be willing to speak at a street corner meeting "as a representative of the unemployed youth." I was surprised and told him I had never spoken publicly; but he urged me on, assuring me that I would do well, and so I agreed. A few days later, standing on a corner in the north end of Winnipeg, I forgot most of what I had so carefully memorized, and so I began repeating what I had so often heard others say. I felt the little crowd around was sympathetic and supportive, and I was quite excited at my apparent success. After that I spoke at several street corner meetings and sometimes addressed Market Square rallies. Thus, I became an activist in the unemployment movement and a regular visitor to the Workers' Centre.

Some of the young people I came to know identified themselves as members of the Young Communist League, or the YCL as it was called. I liked most of them: their ideas, their spirit, and their commitment to what seemed to me to be a very worthy cause. One day one of them approached me, saying: "Comrade, would you like join the YCL?" I enthusiastically accepted, and so became a Young Communist.

In the three years I was a member of the YCL, I never held a designated position, nor did I have any specific responsibility. I was a volunteer activist, doing what had to be done. One day I would distribute literature, another day organize a street corner meeting, occasionally be on a picket line supporting striking workers; but, above all, I loved to speak to the large crowds in the Market Square.

My father's job as an apprentice tailor was short-lived. He found the work incomprehensible and depressing. He simply could not learn the trade. In 1931 there was a modest revival of the Jewish Theatre in Montreal, and he was offered a job, which he happily accepted. The rest of our family remained in Winnipeg, existing on the relief provided by the Welfare Department.

My life had become a boring routine. I was in the doldrums and restless, wanting a more significant role in "the class struggle"; but, above all, wanting a paying job. In Winnipeg that was hopeless, and so I decided to go to Toronto, where I was told "the action" was. At the Winnipeg stockyard I managed to arrange to go east on a cattle train, riding in the caboose in return for helping to feed the cattle.

The train moved slowly, stopping frequently to unload cattle or feed them. I had to help herd the cattle into the corals beside the tracks. We were scheduled to stop for several hours at White River, Ontario, and, after finishing my chores, I wandered down the street beside the tracks. On one side were several buildings, one with the familiar red triangle and the letters YMCA. I entered and found a large comfortable looking room. There were several large old arm chairs and a fireplace with some logs burning. A player piano was tuned to one of Chopin's nocturnes. There was no one else in the room and the chairs were inviting. I sat down, and comforted by the warmth and the music I was soon asleep. When I awoke there were more logs on the fire and the music had stopped; but there was still no one there. I walked back to the train.

Years later, as a union official, I often travelled by train and whenever I passed White River I never failed to look for the "Y" across the tracks. I never forgot the town, and the impression of security and warmth I had sensed in it.

Finally, I arrived in Toronto. At first I stayed with some people I knew, but after a week I was on my own. Getting a job, even in return for just room and board, was hopeless. Unaware that some church missions, the Salvation Army, and soup kitchens provided food and shelter, I devised my own system for survival.

I soon realized that buildings under construction provided a place to sleep. Obtaining food was more difficult. Several times I tried begging or bumming, but it was a degrading experience, and I gave it up for another method. In those days people who could afford it had milk and bread delivered to their homes and left at the door early in the morning. Along quiet streets I would take a bottle of milk from one door and a loaf of bread from another. I never did this when there was only one bottle or one loaf. I managed to eat and my conscience did not bother me.

One damp and cold day I found the Toronto Reference Library on College Street and I went in to warm up. Seeing the racks of books I took one to look at while I sat down at a long table. Soon I was no longer cold. Several days later I went back and that time selected a book on early philosophy. I read with increasing interest and on subsequent visits began to make notes and search the dictionary for the meaning of words that were new to me. While I stayed in Toronto, the Reference Library became my sanctuary and my university — the only university I ever attended.

Another discovery was that the Salvation Army on Jarvis Street provided facilities for washing clothes. After several weeks of sleeping in dust and roaming the streets, my clothes had become very dirty, to say the least, and so I was glad to go to the "Sally Ann" to do my washing. There I learned of the existence of soup kitchens and other places where I could get food. An elderly man was next to me washing his clothes. We struck up a conversation and he offered to take me to these places; he was obviously an experienced "line-stander." We went first to a soup kitchen that was to be open for an hour, and we waited patiently. When it opened we were among the first to receive our grub, which we downed quickly so we could rush to another soup kitchen for a second helping. In the evening my friend took me to the Parliament Mission on Parliament Street. There, with many others, we were given sandwiches and weak cocoa, and then allowed to sleep on the floor. It was not bad, compared to other places where I had slept; at least it was not as cold.

At this point I had given up looking for work, and I spent several weeks eating in soup kitchens, sleeping at the Mission, washing my clothes at the Salvation Army, and reading in the Reference Library. Then I decided to go to Windsor, which was at least warmer than Toronto; and there I ran into double luck. First, I got a job in a large department store as a shoe salesman, working for a month during a bankruptcy sale. Secondly, I found the job had certain advantages. When a sale was made we took the customer's money to the cashier. If there were a number of people in the store and a customer gave me the correct change, I got in the habit of putting the money in my pocket and immediately serving another customer. Sometimes I seemed to forget to give the first customer's money to the cashier, and during the month I did very well indeed. My next job was at a gas station washing cars, but this lasted only two weeks and was not as lucrative. Soon, I was again unemployed.

One day in Windsor I attended a meeting at which the unemployed were voicing their protests and demands. A minor disturbance developed and the police charged in to disperse the crowd. A number of people were arrested, and, as I was standing at the foot of the platform, I was among them. We were charged with disturbing the peace. At the police station I gave an assumed name and said I was 20 years old, although actually I was only 17. I doubt whether the officer believed me. The next day a man who identified himself as a welfare officer came to see me and offered to help. He assured me he was not a police officer, and said I could speak to him in complete confidence. He questioned the name I had given and my age, and finally I told him the truth.

The following day I was released and told to go directly to the City Hall to see the Mayor, David Croll, a man who later became well known in labour circles as Ontario's Minister of Labour, and still later as a member of the Senate. Mayor Croll seemed to know all about me and my father and where we lived. Sternly, but kindly, he told me to go home. He said he had arranged for my transportation to Winnipeg on a cattle train, and said I should be at the stockyard that afternoon. As I was about to leave he took a five dollar bill from his pocket and gave it to me, emphasizing: "Be sure to leave today, and when you get to Winnipeg get in touch with Alderman Gray and inform him of your return." I assured him I would. That night I left Windsor; but I did not return to Winnipeg, instead I went to Montreal where my parents had moved.

In Montreal I got a job in a ladies' hat factory. The pay was three dollars for the first week, and then an additional dollar a week. Understandably I took the job, but after the sixth week there were no more additional dollars. This was before a union was established in the industry. I worked hard and learned the trade fairly quickly.

In Montreal I became acquainted with a few Young Communist League members, but saw them only occasionally. Then the hat factory closed, and once more I was out of work. But, for the first time, I did not mind; I was anxious to return to Winnipeg and again become involved in the workers' movement. And so I went west.

Shortly after I arrived back in Winnipeg, in spring 1932, I was fortunate enough to get a job with a furrier. I rented a small attic room in the home of a family named Harrison and settled down. For several months life was much improved. I liked my job and visited the Workers' Centre regularly to see my comrades.

I was happy in the Harrison's home. They were a third generation Ukrainian-Canadian family; besides the parents there were four sons and two daughters. The eldest of the two girls was Anne. I liked her, and thought she liked me. We soon became good friends and sometimes I invited her downtown to the Workers' Centre. We talked a good deal, and although she was still in high school, she was quite well aware of the problems of unemployment. We shared similar views about the world we were living in. It was the beginning of a life-long relationship. Two years later, in 1934, we were married.

The legacy of the 1919 Winnipeg General Strike, the large number of unemployed, the dismal provisions of public relief, and the widespread cosmopolitan background of its citizens made the Winnipeg of 1932 a city of militant protest. Mass rallies, demonstrations, and strikes were almost daily events, and I took part. One day, when I was not working, I joined a picket line of strikers at the Wellwood Box Factory. I recall the boss sitting at the factory gate with a shot gun across his knees. He had an ominous appearance and I was sure he was quite prepared to use his gun.

On one occasion during the strike the police arrived to escort a group of scabs into the plant. This had happened before, but this time we were determined not to let them in. A fight erupted and I was among those seized by the police. As we were being herded to the paddy wagon I suddenly remembered that my jacket pockets were full of stones; and I realized I might be charged with "carrying concealed weapons." Thinking fast I took off my coat and, making sure a policeman heard me, handed it to one of the strikers, asking him to take it to my mother. Once more I was charged with disturbing the peace. In the jail cells that night we sang such songs as "Hold the Fort" and "The Red Flag" loud and clear.

A day or two later we were taken to court and lined up before Judge Stubbs. He questioned each man, but in a patient and kindly manner. When it came my turn he looked at me over his spectacles for what seemed a long time, and then spoke:

"Young man, are you employed in the Wellwood Box Factory?" he asked.

"No sir," I replied.

"If you are not employed in the factory you were not on strike, then why were you on the picket line?"

"I was supporting the strikers."

"Were you disturbing the peace?"

"No sir," I replied, rather emphatically.

He paused, wrote something in a book, looked at me again, and then, rather impatiently, ruled "Case dismissed." In later years Judge Stubbs left the bench and became active in politics, running as a candidate for the CCF.

After a few months I was laid off by the furrier, and, unable to pay my rent, I planned on going to stay at the Workers' Centre. Ma Harrison would hear nothing of this; her husband was the only one working, but she insisted I keep my room and eat with the family, and I gratefully accepted her kindness.

In fall 1932 I was still without a job and Bill Ross, a leader of the Young Communist League, asked if I would be willing to go to Arborg, some 60 miles north of Winnipeg, to assist farmers in preventing the sale of farms by public auction for non-payment of land taxes. This was a time when the farmers of western Canada were the victims of economic conditions. Long periods of drought, very depressed prices for farm products, and the lack of credit to buy seed or cattle feed, all made it impossible for them to pay their taxes, and so their farms were being seized and sold by auction. In the hope of helping them I agreed to go.

For a time I worked on an Arborg farm, then one day it was announced that a farm in the neighborhood was to be sold for taxes. The farmer for whom I was working became highly incensed at such brutal treatment. He assembled his farm hands and told us something had to be done to stop such sales. He had a plan and instructed us to go around and ask farmers nearby to attend the auction, prepared to help block the sale, one way or another.

When the day came, the auction room was packed with farmers who were sympathetic to the victim and determined to give their support. Soon the auctioneer arrived, a short neatly-dressed man wearing a bowler hat. With him was a tall, young, Royal Canadian Mounted Police constable, wearing the traditional scarlet. Just as the auctioneer was about to begin my employer took the floor. Speaking Ukrainian, he waved his arms and pointed an accusing finger, first at the auctioneer and then at the constable. He went on for about 15 minutes, urging the farmers not to make a bid on the property. The farmers were delighted; they applauded and cheered. The auctioneer understood Ukrainian, but the constable did not understand a word of what was going on.

I was at the back of the room, and as soon as my employer finished I spoke in English. There were loud and long cheers. One farmer tried unsuccessfully to make himself heard; but his words were lost. The auctioneer tried to speak, but the noise was too much for him. Finally, he picked up his briefcase and, still accompanied by the constable, left the hall. The cheers were even louder than before and the sale was called off.

Encouraged by this victory, it was decided to organize a protest march to Winnipeg to present the farmers' grievances to Premier John Bracken. Having shown some initiative in the affair of the sale, I was invited to be a member of a committee of three to organize and lead the march. I was both thrilled and honoured by such a challenging responsibility. After all, I was practically a stranger in the community and very young. It was the first time I had held such a leadership role, and with some emotion I accepted. I believed deeply that the march was a significant step in the farmers' struggle for justice.

We spent the next few days organizing support and making plans with all the precision of a military operation. On the day of the march about 50 farmers assembled, some with knapsacks on their backs and others carrying bags. Members of their families were there to see them off. The youngest of the marchers was 16 and the oldest 70. There was a great deal of excitement as we lined up, five abreast, and started the long trek.

We planned to walk about 20 miles a day, and stop at designated places to rest, eat, and sleep. We received generous contributions of food and these supplies, with blankets and personal belongings, were carried in a truck which I had managed to borrow. The truck went ahead to complete arrangements for eating and sleeping. Usually, farm women along the way prepared a hot meal. Some of us slept in nearby homes and others on the floor of the building in which we were fed. Every morning there was a hot breakfast of boiled potatoes, chucks of bacon, homemade bread, and coffee, a typical breakfast for farmers in the area. The noon meal and snacks were prepared by the group in the truck. As we marched along the road, we were joined by other farmers, and when we reached Winnipeg on the sixth day our delegation had grown to over 100.

On the grounds of the Manitoba legislative building a large crowd had gathered to greet us. There was much shouting, hand-shaking, and the usual speeches, including fiery addresses by Bill Ross and Joe Forkin. My memory is hazy about what happened after. A delegation met the Premier; but I was not a member. In some ways I was satisfied to be one of the crowd and happy with my part in such a memorable adventure, but in other ways I was disappointed to have been passed over.

After the farmers' march I was once more at a loose end and decided to go to Regina with Harry Binder who was moving there as a full-time YCL organizer. The YCL gave me the names of some comrades who might help me find work. On the way there I had a rather amusing experience. I caught a freight train leaving Winnipeg and found an empty box car, which I crawled in. Knowing the danger of being locked in, I jammed the door so it could not be shut from the outside. Then I wrapped myself in a blanket and fell asleep. The next thing I knew was that the train had stopped at some prairie station, and there was a loud voice shouting at me. "Hey, what the hell are you doing here? Get out."

I crawled out to be confronted by the weather-beaten red face of a railway policeman. He shouted at me again, and I told him I was sleeping. "I don't want to see you around here again, now get out," he shouted.

I responded in my most reasonable voice: "Officer, if you would be kind enough not to look at me, you would not see me." As he turned and walked away I thought I caught the glimmer of a faint smile; in any event, he did not look back, and as the train began to move I climbed back into the box car.

There was no work in Regina, and so I went to Saskatoon, then to Moose Jaw, and after that to a farm in Donavon, Saskatchewan. This was an area that had been hit by a long devastating drought. The farmer I went to see about work told me his two sons had gone to the city looking for work. There were chores to be done and I could have room and board for helping, but there was no money. About three weeks later his sons returned and so I left. The farmer gave me a few dollars to tide me over, and back in Regina I rented a small room from one of the comrades.

Once again I started looking for work; but there was none. It was early 1933, and at the age of 18 I was just one of hundreds of young men who were drifting about the country. My spirit was weakening and my enthusiasm diminishing. With only public school education and no trade there were no prospects for work, despite the assurances of politicians that "prosperity is just around the corner."

During this time, as a spectator, I attended the founding convention of the Co-operative Commonwealth Federation (CCF) held in Regina in July 1933. There, despite some confusion in my mind, I listened with great interest to the speeches of J.S. Woodsworth, M.J. Coldwell, T.C. Douglas, and others. Slowly, I began to realize that there were views regarding solutions to the great social problems other than those I held.

Then, one day, I was asked to meet with some of the Young Communist League leaders, including my friend, Harry Binder. There were four of them at the meeting, and they seemed unusually serious. The atmosphere in the room was ominous. Without any preliminary remarks one of them asked if I had any contact with Trotskyites, needless to say, I was surprised at the question.

"Why do you ask me that?" I asked.

"We have reason to believe that you are associating with Trotskyites, or that you are one of them," another accused me.

I denied this emphatically. They then asked if I had been reading Trotskyite literature, and again I denied it.

There was a brief silence as the comrades looked at each other. I realized I was facing some sort of a trial, and I did not like it at all. Slowly, Harry Binder opened his briefcase and took out a copy of the publication *The Militant*, the official organ of the Trotskyite organization in the United States. Triumphantly, he held it up for all to see, and then, turning to me, said: "Comrade, this was found in your room."

I had completely forgotten that I had just received the paper from a Montreal friend. When it arrived I had put it on the bureau in my room, and had not given it another thought. I was terribly embarrassed at having denied reading Trotskyite literature. The newspaper was mine, and the fact that I had not read it was hardly believable. But what if I had read it? Surely that would not make me a Trotskyite. The comrades were not convinced. They thought I was lying, and finally they told me that, in the opinion of the Young Communist League, I was "a Trotskyite and a Revisionist," and thus "an enemy of the working class." There was no place for me in the YCL.

I was shocked. I had a faint idea of what a Trotskyite was, but no idea of what being terms "a Revisionist" implied; and being called "an enemy of the working class" upset me terribly. Young, impressionistic, and idealistic, I was disappointed that my comrades, who knew so much more about the world than I did, and to whom I looked for guidance and inspiration, should call me "an enemy of the working class."

In any event, my association with the YCL had ended. I left the meeting confused and sad. A few days later I climbed aboard a box car and headed for Montreal. As the incidents and experiences of my life began to unfold a kind of emotional reflex, both sentimental and anger, welled up inside me.

CHAPTER TWO
Learning about Unions

A FEW WEEKS AFTER ARRIVING in Montreal, I got a job in a ladies' hat factory. Several months earlier the United Hat, Cap and Millinery Workers' Union (AFL-TLC) had succeeded in organizing workers in the millinery industry and establishing collective bargaining. I joined the union and soon became interested and increasingly involved in its activities; in due course becoming a union officer.

The historical background of the United Hatters is typical of unions in the needle trades. A majority of the workers were women, most of whom worked in small factories. Others performed "piece work" in their homes, which were known as "bedroom shops." These women were completely at the mercy of their employers, who arbitrarily decided the rates for each piece of work. In some cases there were more "hands" working in bedroom shops than in the factory.

Efforts to organize unions had met with determined and often brutal resistance by the employers. There were immediate dismissals and the blacklisting of so-called troublemakers, making it impossible for them to get a job anywhere in the industry. When unions did succeed in organizing the workers, the employer most frequently refused to meet with union representatives to negotiate a collective agreement. When the workers went on strike and set up picket lines, the police protected strike-breakers and frequently dispersed the pickets, beating some and arresting others. Employers who were unable to get sufficient police protection hired their own "goon squads." The courts showed little sympathy to strikers and frequently granted injunctions against picketing. Fines imposed on the Hatters' Union at times threatened its very existence.

The history of the United Hatters, like that of the International Ladies' Garment Workers' Union, the Amalgamated Clothing Workers, and other needle trades organizations, is filled with sad chapters in the development of today's industrial relations system.

The first recorded efforts at organizing the hat and cap industry in Montreal date back to 1923. At that time the union assigned J.B. Salsberg to undertake an organizing campaign. He was a young, energetic, and competent organizer, but, for a number of reasons, his efforts were unsuccessful. Later, other attempts were made. At one point a rather militant strike took place, but again management resistance and the lack of union spirit which prevailed in the Province of Quebec at the time, prevented the union from becoming established.

In late 1933 there was another attempt, this time headed by Louis Fine of Toronto, who was later to become one of the country's foremost mediators. Fine's suave manner, his quiet but very logical and pragmatic approach, impressed the leading employers. They took the position, however, that they would be willing to sign a collective agreement only if certain conditions were met: first, that workers demonstrate that they really desired a union; and second, that should an agreement result in changes and improved working conditions, such improvements would apply to the industry as a whole, thus avoiding any employer being placed at a disadvantage.

Fine accepted the logic of this argument and with others, notably his deputy, Maurice Silcoff, initiated an energetic campaign in which most of the factories in Montreal were organized. When negotiations were concluded the conditions in the agreement became applicable throughout the industry, under the terms of the Quebec Labour Agreements Extension Act. One of the provisions in the agreement was the establishment of a joint committee, consisting of an equal number of union and management representatives, to assure that all factories covered by the agreement lived up to the conditions specified.

After several months working as a clocker, I was elected a shop steward for the union, an honour and trust which I gladly accepted. The duties included looking after the grievances of the workers, which were many. These were discussed with the employer, and if I could not get a satisfactory settlement I would call on Maurice Silcoff, who had become manager of the union. He usually lost little time in getting to the plant, and if he was not personally available he would assign his assistant, Paul Fournier.

I took greater and greater interest in union affairs, attending meetings and often taking part in discussions. I had a feeling, however, that something was missing, and that the union should undertake some cultural and educational activities. After discussing this with some of my colleagues, and receiving assurance of their support, I told Silcoff I would like to appear before the Executive Board of the union to make this suggestion. I was invited to a meeting where I outlined my ideas, and said that, while I had no blueprint, I would be glad to prepare a proposal if the Board approved. I was asked to wait outside while the members discussed the idea. Eventually, I was told that, while the Board appreciated my interest and initiative, the union, being in a formative stage, was preoccupied with a variety of industrial problems and the launching of such a programme was considered premature. I was disappointed, but bore no malice and carried on as a shop steward.

Sometime later, as I became better known, I was asked whether I would be interested in running for the office of recording secretary. I said I would be happy to, but only if there were no other candidates. I did not want to become involved in any kind of competition. When the election of officers came around mine was the only name put forward for the position, and so I became the recording secretary. I felt I had attained a leadership position of some importance.

The office required me to attend not only the Executive Board meetings, but also meetings of various committees, and to prepare minutes of the discussions. I carried my papers in a briefcase which I took to work each morning — a badge of office. My colleagues often looked at me, no doubt wondering about the new posture I had developed.

In due course, I again raised the matter of educational and cultural programmes at an Executive Board meeting, and this time I had no difficulty in getting acceptance. The matter was left entirely in my hands. The programme I initiated was a simple one. It consisted first of short seminars to be held twice a month, between 5:30 and 7:00 o'clock in the evening. Secondly, the formation of a choral group. Third, the publication of a monthly mimeographed bulletin, of which I became writer, editor, and printer. The choral group was placed in the hands of one of the members with a musical background.

I assumed responsibility for organizing the seminars; but the first effort was almost disastrous. We invited Alex Edmunson, a well-known literary figure in Montreal and later a professor at Carleton University, Ottawa, to conduct a session on public speaking at the union headquarters. Notice of the seminar, with an invitation to all interested to attend, was published in our bulletin. On the appointed night Edmunson appeared. We chatted for a time and then, to my horror, I realized that not a single person had appeared. At first I thought they might come late, but they did not.

In the union hall was a room where members gathered after work to play cards, almost a ritual in any needle trades union headquarters. I went to Maurice Silcoff and told him what had happened. I asked him to go to the card room with me to urge some of the card players to come to our seminar. They thought the exercise was rather amusing, but they agreed to help out and soon the chairs were filled.

Edmunson delivered a short talk and then invited someone to come to the front to demonstrate how they spoke publicly. No one volunteered. He finally convinced one member of the audience to come forward. He seemed a bit frightened and said he had nothing to talk about. Edmunson suggested he tell a joke. Oh, he had many jokes, this chap said, but this was hardly the time or place for the kind of jokes he told. Edmunson told him to go ahead anyway, and he did. From that moment it was not difficult to get someone to come forward with jokes or stories. The atmosphere was exciting and the language so phosphorous that it would have embarrassed a group of sailors. Edmunson took it all in his stride and seemed to enjoy it. In a very serious and constructive fashion he evaluated the manner in which the stories were told.

That was our first experience in recruiting students. We changed our methods by involving shop stewards and were fairly successful in getting larger numbers of workers to attend. The programme continued for a long time.

Though I was only 20, the duties of recording secretary included representing the local on various bodies, such as the Montreal Trades and Labour Council and the Quebec Federation of Labour. I recall that late in 1940, Tom Moore, the president of the Trades and Labour Congress of Canada, came to Montreal to address a meeting of the Labour Council. He was known to be a fluent and eloquent speaker; but shortly after he began his address his speech became progressively slower. His words began to slur and run together. Those in the audience, wondering what was happening, began talking to each other. Moore, with one hand holding the table beside which he stood, tried to carry on; but he could not be heard above the hum of the audience. Eventually, he was gently led off the platform and then rushed to the hospital. He never recovered from the attack and died some months later.

In 1939 I was, for the first time, a delegate to the convention of the Trades and Labour Congress of Canada, which was held in London, Ontario. I was then 24 and still impressionable, idealistic, and rather naive about the stresses and strains that existed within the labour movement. Many of the matters that came before the convention were strange and confusing to me, and soon forgotten.

But there was one issue which was discussed with a great deal of emotion, and sometimes anger, which I have never forgotten, not to this day. A serious split had occurred in the labour movement in the United States, where unions affiliated to the newly-formed Congress of Industrial Organizations (CIO) were in conflict with the American Federation of Labour (AFL). The older AFL considered these CIO unions, which were mainly organized on an industrial rather than a craft basis, to be dual unions, in competition with the longer-established unions belonging to the AFL.

The president of the AFL and the presidents of a number of international unions wanted these competing organizations expelled from the TLC. They had issued an ultimatum that, unless the TLC took such action, the per-capita payments which were made to the Canadian body would be cut off. The TLC was dependent on this revenue, and the leadership capitulated, recommending to the convention that seven industrial unions be expelled.

Carl Berg of the Hod Carriers' International Union was the chairman of the Resolutions Committee and it was his duty to place the recommendation before the convention. He was a bulky man, and sitting motionless and stiffly behind the long platform table he gave the appearance of a bust placed on the table. His deep voice, with a slight Swedish accent, came through the loudspeakers in slowly measured words that sounded like a sledge hammer pounding at the very heart and limbs of the labour movement. Several times he paused as his emotions built up. He was visibly moved by the disagreeable task, and when he finished reading the resolution and moved concurrence, he left the platform and broke down and cried.

I was bewildered and confused. I did not really understand the meaning of dual unions or the relevance of "in opposition to the AFL." Expelling workers and their unions from the national labour movement for such incomprehensible reasons was contrary to what I so passionately believed. I have always regarded the unity and solidarity of the labour movement with reverence, and indeed as being the corner-stone of its strength. I could not understand or support a proposal to divide the labour movement. I wanted to speak out and enquire why we were being asked to expel workers from our ranks. Why were we being asked, in a few minutes, to destroy that which labour men and women had struggled to build for more than 100 years? Such were my innermost feelings, but I sat in silence. It would be many years before that breach was healed.

The same year the world became engulfed in a unprecedented war. Adolf Hitler and his Nazis, in the leprosy of their minds, unleashed violence and horror that knew no bounds. This brought a quick recovery from the Great Depression of the earlier 1930s. New industries mushroomed and old industries expanded, all geared to the war effort that taxed them to their very limits. With thousands of young men in the armed forces there was a serious shortage of labour. More and more women entered the work force in roles previously regarded as men's work, thus "Rosie the Riveter" was born.

When the war ended, the spectacular advances in technology and science, developed during the conflict, were applied to peacetime production, transforming the very nature of industrial life. There were new concepts and methods of production, and new words, "cybernetics" and "automation," creating fear and anxiety for working people. Others argued that the scientific and technological developments represented "progress," and that in the long run all would benefit.

Trade-union development was equally dramatic. Labour laws were liberalized and the right of workers to organize and bargain collectively received legal recognition. These rights became more secure and legislation was influenced when the International Labour Organization adopted its Convention 87 on "Freedom of Association and the Right to Organize," and then, in 1949, Convention 98 on "Right to Organize and Collective Bargaining."

Improved labour legislation, coupled with a buoyant economy and the emergence of the CIO organizing mass production industries, made it possible for the labour movement in Canada to increase its membership from about 250,000 in 1939 to over 1,000,000 in 1955.

The Province of Quebec had changed from an agricultural to an industrial society. The influx of people from rural areas to Montreal and other industrial centres, and the employment of thousands of workers in new war industries, had brought about greater interest and often militant demands by workers for union representation. In part to meet this demand, the Montreal Trades and Labour Council, in 1942, established a Metal Trades Council as an umbrella organization made up of representatives of various metal trades unions. The purpose was to organize workers in war production plants and channel them into the various unions that had jurisdiction in such industries. Robert Haddow, an international representative of the International Association of Machinists (IAM), was chairman of the Council and the driving force in the organizing campaign.

Soon after its establishment the Council sent an appeal to all unions in the province for financial or other assistance. The Hatters' Union offered my services for one month, with payment of my salary, which was about $120. Haddow provided me with a list of Defence Industries Limited (DIL) munitions plants in the province and told me to begin organizing them. It was a new experience, but one I approached with confidence. The DIL plant at Verdun was producing a variety of cartridges and had more than 3,000 employees. Because of the many skilled and semi-skilled machinists and trained inspectors employed there, it was generally accepted in the labour movement that Verdun was clearly in the jurisdiction of the Machinists. Haddow asked me to start there.

It was in May 1942 that I prepared a leaflet and handed it out at the plant gate. Announcing the start of the campaign, it listed the benefits of union organization and outlined the union's objectives once it became the bargaining agent. Finally, it invited the Verdun workers to join the union by signing an application card and paying an initiation fee of one dollar.

While I was handing out the leaflets, I managed to speak to some of the workers. Any who showed a particular interest were invited to meet me at the lunch break or after working hours. I realized that alone it would be very difficult for me to get a majority to join what we named the Provisional Union Organizing Committee. They were given application cards and receipt books and asked to sign up as many members as they could in their respective departments. In the first week, 16 of these volunteers signed up over 400; it was a good beginning.

Going to the plant every day I soon found that the best time to talk with the people was during the lunch break. In the morning they were rushing into the plant, and in the evening they were anxious to get home. From discussions with members of the committee I learned quite a lot about working conditions in the plant. I asked what specific conditions needed improvement and what the union should try to obtain once we started bargaining. Their recommendations varied widely from higher wages to sanitary conditions.

The second circular was more specific about the union's programme, and it also announced that I would be seeking an appointment with the plant manager to introduce him to our union and its activities. This announcement was well received: it sort of legitimized our union.

In mid-June I arranged to meet the plant manager, H.B. Hanna. When I arrived at the plant I was admitted by a security guard, then escorted by another guard to the manager's office. As we walked through the plant I waved to some of the workers I knew and spoke briefly to others. Later, I learned the visit had reverberated through the plant.

At the time of our meeting, federal legislation making collective bargaining mandatory under certain conditions had just been enacted. Nevertheless, I was curious about the company's reaction to our campaign. I told Hanna of the union's efforts to organize employees in war production factories and expressed the hope that the DIL management would not discourage workers from joining the union. I explained that the IAM had already granted a charter to the Verdun DIL local.

Hanna said it was company policy neither to discourage nor to encourage their employees to join or not to join a union. The company would respect the wishes of the majority of its employees. He added as a personal note that if there was to be a union in the plant, he hoped a substantial majority would become members so there would be no friction. I told him his hopes were more than likely to be realized. Finally, he drew my attention to the difficulties in getting substantial wage increases because of the provisions of the wartime wage and price control legislation. In a friendly, and somewhat fatherly, fashion he tried to caution me against making too many promises and commitments to workers. Our discussion ended on a surprisingly friendly note.

In the fourth week of the campaign I issued another circular with a brief account of the meeting with Hanna, and announcing that we would shortly apply to the Department of Labour for certification as bargaining agent. The circular was effective in encouraging others to sign up.

As my one-month assignment with the Metals Trades Council was about to end I was, with sadness, getting ready to return to my job in the hat factory. Then Haddow told me my assignment could be extended for another month, or even two, if I was interested.

In addition to trying to develop the union at Verdun, we planned to begin organizing the DIL plant at Valleyfield, about 40 miles south of Montreal, where there were some 3,000 employees. I went to Valleyfield several times and spoke to workers at the plant gate, managing to interest a few of them. However, we decided that, until our union was certified at Verdun, and a collective agreement negotiated, our organizing efforts at Valleyfield would be low-keyed.

On 11 August 1942, the certification vote was held at Verdun with the balloting under the supervision of the federal Department of Labour. The question on the ballot was: "Are you in favour of the company negotiating an agreement with the Metal Trades Council as the sole bargaining agent for DIL Verdun employees?" There were 3,230 workers who voted "Yes" and 320 who voted "No." Naturally, we were delighted and thrilled by the result of this historic vote and the overwhelming majority who had supported us.

Because the Verdun local was chartered by the International Association of Machinists, and more particularly because I had no previous collective bargaining experience, and certainly not on such a scale, Haddow and another IAM organizer, Adrien Villeneuve, joined the negotiating committee and myself and were the principal spokesmen for the union.

In the course of the negotiations, I was often lost in the maze of unfamiliar craft and contract terminology. Most of the time I just listened and I was very impressed with the give-and-take, the proposals and counter-proposals, and the compromises that were made. While it was confusing, I realized how little I knew and how much I had to learn about this strange and complicated business called collective bargaining.

The negotiations were unusually brief, and after only three formal sessions, the agreement in principle was initiated. On Sunday, 23 August, a mass meeting was held in the plant canteen to ratify the draft agreement. A number of recommendations were made and several subsequent sessions with the company were necessary before the contract was worked out in a manner satisfactory to both parties. Finally, on 3 September, the contract was formally signed. It was a great day for me, and I felt a tremendous sense of accomplishment. It was with a new feeling of purpose and confidence that I set out on my new assignment, the organization of the DIL workers at Valleyfield.

There, I rented a room in a store across the street from the plant to use as the union office. As before, I set up a Provisional Campaign Committee, composed of some of the workers I had got to know. They were equipped with application cards and receipt books and asked to recruit members. We distributed a circular announcing the successful completion of negotiations at Verdun and listing gains the union had made. The Valleyfield workers were urged to follow that example by signing up with the union.

The circular created a good deal of excitement and the response to our appeal was far beyond our expectations. The day after the circular appeared we received about 200 signed application cards. As the momentum of the campaign increased, the membership grew rapidly. Some days workers stood in long lines outside the union office, waiting their turn to sign up and pay the one-dollar initiation fee. I had not seen such enthusiastic support for a union before, nor have I since.

It seemed as if the whole town knew about the union. Initially, I was a stranger in Valleyfield, but, as in all small communities, strangers quickly become known and identified. Wherever I went there was support and encouragement from the people. When the time came to pay the rent for our union office the elderly store owner, speaking somewhat awkwardly, but with sincere humility, said there was no charge for the first month, that was his contribution to the union. Such was the spirit of the people of Valleyfield in fall 1942.

About a month after our campaign began, a majority of the workers had joined our union and we were in a position to apply for certification. We established a formal structure by electing officers and committees. However, on the matter of obtaining a union charter we ran into difficulties.

I had assumed that the IAM would charter the local, as it had at Verdun, but this was not the case. I was told that, because of the nature of the production at Valleyfield, it was not within the Machinists' jurisdiction.

I was advised to apply to the Trades and Labour Congress at Ottawa for what was known as a "federal charter." The situation was that when a group of workers wanted to join a union, but none of the unions affiliated to the TLC claimed jurisdiction of such an operation, then the TLC could issue its own charter and the local would be identified as a "federal union" of the TLC.

Needless to say, all this was very confusing to me. I had never heard of federal unions, none existed in Quebec. Nevertheless, I arranged an appointment with then acting president of the Congress, Percy Bengough, to make application for such a charter. I little knew what that meeting would lead to.

CHAPTER THREE
From the Shop to the Field

ON THE TRAIN TO OTTAWA I was completely absorbed in thoughts about my imminent meeting with the president of the TLC. I tried to visualize the kind of reception I would get, his reaction to our request for a charter, the questions he might ask. Those three hours seemed endless and I had mixed feelings about what was to prove to be an eventful journey.

In Ottawa I went directly to the TLC headquarters, in a stately old McLaren street residence converted into an office. During the short taxi ride from the station, I was still thinking about the possible results of the meeting. The receptionist seemed to be expecting me and at once opened the door to the president's office. Except for a well-polished old oak desk and three matching armchairs that half-circled the front of the desk, the office looked more like an old-fashioned living room.

Percy Bengough was an impressive man: tall and heavy-shouldered, he had long arms and extraordinarily large hands. He had light gray sparse hair and expressive small eyes that mirrored his moods. His ready smile was like that of a young boy.

Born in England, he had served his apprenticeship as a machinist and had originally joined the Amalgamated Society of Engineers, a British union which had branches in Canada. It was later absorbed by the International Association of Machinists. Coming to Canada he settled in Vancouver and established the reputation of being a militant and effective trade unionist, becoming secretary-treasurer of the Vancouver Trades and Labour Council. Outside the labour movement his greatest interest was in collecting coins. He became an outstanding numismatist and attended conventions of collectors both in Canada and the United States. One of his greatest enjoyments was to show his albums to friends and relate the story behind individual pieces.

I liked Percy Bengough the moment we met. He did not have an effervescent personality, nor was he pretentious or overbearing. Everything about him seemed unhurried, quiet, and solid. As we talked, his balanced temperament, his slow but steady movements, and his soft deep voice had a warm and soothing effect. The anxiety and nervousness that had possessed me during the trip seemed to have melted away. I was at ease, relaxed, and comfortable. This was a kind and modest man of sincerity, strength, and wisdom. No man I ever knew influenced my life more profoundly than did Percy Bengough.

At first we discussed the social and political situation in Quebec. We talked about the volatile leadership of the controversial Premier, Maurice Duplessis, and about the charismatic Minister of Labour, Antonio Barrett, who, like Bengough, was a member of the IAM, and whom Bengough described as "a level headed bloke."

Then we turned to the purpose of my visit, which was, as he knew, the issuance of a TLC charter for the DIL local in Valleyfield. He did not hesitate, ask questions, or comment. Unceremoniously, he merely said, "Of course," and that was all. He asked me to leave the names of the local union's officers with his secretary and said a charter would be mailed in a few days. The questions that had been on my mind for days were thus quickly settled. I was both relieved and gratified.

Obviously, he knew of the energetic drive of the revitalized labour movement in Quebec, organizing new industries. He asked fundamental questions about the campaign and then enquired about my job in the hat factory, my activities in the Hatters' Union, and the duration of my assignment with the Metal Trades Council.

As I replied to his questions, I had the feeling that his thoughts had wandered from what I was saying. Momentarily he seemed detached, as if he was thinking of other things. Then, with an abrupt U-turn in the conversation, he asked: "Would you be interesting in working full-time for the Congress?" I was stunned; my thoughts raced in all directions, and for a moment I was unable to answer. Then, to be sure I had heard him correctly and that I understood the question, I asked him what he had in mind.

He said he was interested in involving the Congress in general organizing activities. Many of the new industries did not fall within the jurisdiction of affiliated unions, and he wanted them organized into groups federally chartered by the TLC. "And so," he repeated, "I am asking if you are interested in working for the TLC as an organizer in Quebec."

I was most surprised, and it was with some difficulty that I contained my excitement and emotion. I had expected to go back to the grind of my inconsequential job in the hat factory; but here I was, being asked whether I would be interested in working for the TLC in such an important and exciting job. I didn't hesitate, I immediately accepted.

He enquired about my salary with the Metal Trades Council. I told him it was $30 a week, and he said the Congress would give me the same, plus $25 a week for incidental expenses. He then took a sheet of paper and began to write. After a few moments he called in his secretary and gave her the sheet, explaining: "Mr. Swerdlow is going to work for the Congress, these are his credentials. Would you please type this, affix the Congress seal, and bring it back as soon as you can."

I was still surprised. I did not know what to expect. I had no idea what a TLC credential looked like or what it said. While we waited, I asked what industries I should try to organize and where in the province I should begin. He paused, and then with a whimsical expression replied in slow, soft, and measured words:

"Max, you will be the TLC representative in Quebec. This means the entire province is your territory. Where you should begin to organize is for you to decide. What industries you should organize is also something for you to decide. On such questions, it would be better that you advise me, rather than I advise you."

He paused again: "However, I expect that in the main you will be organizing industries that can be directly chartered by the Congress."

I did not expect, nor was I sure I wanted that kind of a reply. I expected specific instructions, guidance, and advice. I had mixed feelings yet I felt very proud, for just four months earlier I was pulling steamed felt hoods off hot metal dies in a ladies' hat factory; and here I was now, the Quebec representative of the TLC and I was expected to advise the president. How important I felt.

Soon the secretary returned with my credential. He read the document and, after signing it in large decisive characters he handed it to me. It was impressive, typed on TLC letterhead with a gold seal embossed with the Congress crest. It read: "This is to certify that Mr. M. Swerdlow has been appointed by the Executive Council of the Trades and Labour Congress of Canada as representative and organizer, to organize and establish Federal Unions under the jurisdiction of the Trades and Labour Congress of Canada. Mr. Swerdlow will be the recognized authority of the Trades and Labour Congress of Canada. Given under our hands and seal this Thirtieth Day of November 1942."

I read the second paragraph twice to make sure I was not dreaming; I felt as if my chest had swelled six inches. When it was time for me to leave, I asked when I was expected to return to Ottawa. The President smiled broadly as we shook hands and said, "When you organize another plant." We both laughed, and I said: "Chief, I got the message." In the years that followed, I and all the congress staff affectionately called him "Chief."

I left the Congress headquarters with a very happy heart. I was the first full-time organizer of the TLC. That evening, on the train returning to Montreal, I kept looking at my credential and repeating to myself: "Mr. Swerdlow will be the recognized authority of the Trades and Labour Congress of Canada in any territory to which he may be assigned...." I believe I smiled all the way back; I could hardly wait to get home and tell my wife about it. I was almost bursting with joy.

I returned to Valleyfield with the good news of having obtained a charter. In a few days it arrived and we then applied to the Department of Labour for certification. In the meantime I began preparing a collective agreement to present to the company. This was a new experience, for I knew little about contractual terminology, about the conditions that should be embodied in such a legal document, nor about the possible pitfalls. I felt very concerned about my inadequacy.

I took the agreement that was being negotiated at Verdun and within that framework laboriously began to adapt the agreement to the situation at Valleyfield. Finally, when I had completed the first draft, I discussed it with Haddow and the local union officers. After they had made a number of changes in the text, I asked some colleagues in other unions to assist me in refining the draft into a presentable document. The union was certified in January 1943, and shortly afterward we arranged to meet the company in the plant conference room to begin negotiating an agreement.

On the day of the first session with the company there was a great deal of excitement in the plant. Workers everywhere were discussing and speculating on the outcome of the negotiations. On our way to the conference room, workers greeted and encouraged us: some with broad smiles and others with fingers forming a "V for victory" sign, and even some with clenched fists.

The management representatives were already there. We shook hands and talked briefly before sitting down in the traditional fashion: the union and company representatives facing each other across the table. The environment was relaxed and quite friendly. I started with a brief statement explaining that the 14 employees on the union's negotiating committee represented all the hourly-paid employees in the plant, and that I, as a representative of the Trades and Labour Congress, was there to assist them. I also expressed the hope that a satisfactory agreement would be completed within a reasonably short time. At the conclusion of my remarks I presented the management with several copies of our proposed agreement.

The plant manager then spoke briefly about the company's policy with regard to labour relations. He stressed that DIL had not and would not interfere with the employees' choice of joining or not joining the union. He hoped that a collective agreement would be reached soon and, looking directly at the employees, said: "You and I have an important job to do here, and that is to maintain continuous production as efficiently as possible. That, gentlemen, is our role in the war effort."

When he finished speaking, he gave us all a copy of a collective agreement prepared by the company and, without any further formalities, began to read from the company's text. After he had read several clauses it slowly began to dawn on me that the company's text was being used as the basis for negotiation and that the collective agreement I had so laboriously drafted, with the help of others, had somehow been set aside and ignored.

I interjected politely, saying: "Sir, I believe the procedure we are now following is wrong. We should be examining first the union's proposal, not the company's." The manager, holding up the company's text, replied: "Mr. Swerdlow, this is the company's counter-proposal."

"On what basis," I asked, "do you make a counter-proposal, when in fact you have not heard the union's proposal?" There was mild laughter on our side of the table and the manager, leaning forward with a trace of a "who-are-you-kidding" smile, replied: "Mr. Swerdlow, I have read enough of the circulars you distributed at this plant for the past few months to know what the union will be asking."

"Since when," I asked, "is a union circular considered to be a proposal for a collective agreement?"

He did not reply at once and my question was momentarily suspended in the air. It seemed to have caught him off guard and he seemed slightly embarrassed. It was not my intention to create that kind of a situation, yet I felt an important principle was at stake. After all, it was the union that was making demands on the company, and these were embodied in the union's formal proposal. Therefore, I reasoned, the union text should be the basis for discussion. The manger consulted briefly with his colleagues, and then turning to us said: "Gentlemen, your point is well-taken. I suggest that we examine both texts at the same time."

Not wanting to be difficult or sticky at the very outset of the negotiations, I consulted briefly with the union officers and we agreed to accept the company's suggestion. I was satisfied with the compromise; above all, I did not want to see the first collective agreement I had ever drafted, and of which I was so very proud, disregarded and forgotten.

When we began to examine the company's text we found that, with the exception of wages and some other monetary provisions, it was very similar to ours. I should have expected that, for predictably both the company and the union had based their respective proposals on the Verdun contract, negotiated only a few months before.

Early in 1943, after a number of bargaining sessions, the Valleyfield agreement was signed. That experience gave me a deep sense of accomplishment and gratification. After all, I had organized the workers, I had drafted and negotiated the agreement, and I signed the document on behalf of the TLC. I did not take into account the precedent established in the Verdun negotiations by the IAM. I was very possessive about my first TLC local and my first agreement and I felt that I had arrived in my work in the trade union movement.

After the agreement was signed we proceeded to establish a proper union structure. We elected various committees and shop stewards, and generally put our house in order. However, on the matter of collecting dues from the members, we had a problem. At that time the TLC did not have adequate provision for the collection of dues from members of federally-chartered unions. There was only a small four-page membership card on which the payment of dues was supposed to be recorded by the dues collector. Obviously this system was unworkable in a large sprawling plant with 3,000 members. I could not see how our shop stewards would go about collecting dues, recording the payment in the membership book, and turning the money over to the financial secretary.

And so I obtained a supply of the membership books from Ottawa and distributed them to the members. Then I designed a simple dues stamp, bearing only the TLC crest, and I had a quantity printed. Each month I gave the financial secretary a supply of the stamps, getting a receipt. He then gave each shop steward a supply, and the steward, in turn, gave a stamp to each member who paid the one dollar monthly due. It was not by any means the best system, nor was it foolproof, but it worked reasonably well. In the months that followed I used the same stamps in other locals. Eventually, a checkoff of union dues was introduced in most organized industries in Quebec.

During the first few months as the TLC district representative, my home was also my office. As the workload steadily increased, I realized that, if I were to begin organizing other industries, I would need assistance, and so I arranged a meeting with President Bengough. I took with me a copy of the Valleyfield agreement and showed him the dues stamp, explaining my collection system. He seemed satisfied and a bit amused at this initiative, but he explained that the Congress would have to develop a uniform procedure to be applied nationally for the collection of dues in chartered locals. Meanwhile, I should continue using my system. I was pleased.

I suggested we should not restrict our organizing to war production industries that would close down after the war. We should include permanent industries, such as rubber, meat packing, and chemicals. He was in full agreement with this view.

I went on: "Chief, to undertake this kind of an organizing drive I'll need assistance and some facilities."

"What do you want?" he asked.

"I would like to engage a French-Canadian organizer, rent a modest office, and engage an office secretary, and we will need some office equipment," I replied boldly.

"Max, we don't have a Congress office in any other province," he said.

"Chief," I went on quickly, "Neither do we have a Congress district representative in any other province."

He was silent for a moment, then, leaning back in his chair, he smiled and asked: "How much will it cost?" I told him I didn't know, but I expected the salary for an additional organizer would be the same as mine; and if he approved I would find out about other costs and let him know. He agreed and I returned to Montreal with authorization to hire another organizer.

On the recommendation of some colleagues, I interviewed Rémi Duquette of the Amalgamated Street Railway Union. He was a polite, kind, and generous man with a balanced temperament, a warm smile, and a pleasant disposition. He spoke both French and English fluently, and his enthusiasm and considerable experience in trade union affairs made him an ideal candidate. I was impressed and engaged him immediately.

In due course we rented a small office on Notre Dame Street, bought some second-hand furniture and engaged an office secretary. Then, for the first time, I felt really established and ready to undertake, in a true sense, the exciting job of organizing unions throughout the province.

Rémi and I drew up a list of peacetime industries we intended organizing. It included rubber, meat packaging, can manufacturing, refractories, breweries, sawmills, and many others. It was an ambitious programme. Duquette went to St. Jérôme where the Dominion Rubber and Regent Knitting Mills were located. I undertook to organize the British Rubber plant at Lachine, as well as Canada Packers, Swift's, and the Wilson meat packing plants in Montreal.

It was not long before I realized that organizing these industries was bound to be far more difficult than organizing war production plants. Although many of the workers in these industries joined unions, there were many others who were afraid to join and some who were against unions, at least the kind of union we represented.

In the early 1940s unions in Quebec were usually identified as either international, such as ours, or Canadian, such as those associated with the Canadian and Catholic Confederation of Labour (CCL), which later became the Confederation of National Trade Unions (CNTU). The CCL was a confessional or Catholic Church-oriented organization. Newspapers, politicians, and some employer groups frequently spoke out against what they called "foreign international unions which want to dominate Canadian workers," in reference to the international nature of most of the unions affiliated to the TLC. Moreover, notwithstanding the legislative provisions legitimizing unions and collective bargaining, some employers continued openly resist the organization of their employers. Despite all this, we had considerable success.

In a short time Duquette established good contacts in both Dominion Rubber and Regent Knitting at St. Jérôme. I did the same at the British Rubber and Canada Packers plants. We distributed circulars at the plant gates, held meetings, and signed up members. As the momentum of our organizing drives increased, membership grew rapidly, except at the Regent Knitting Mill. There the management not only discouraged, but intimidated workers against joining. We carried on with our campaign, despite the company's hostility and disregard for the law.

About four months after our organizing drive began in the four plants, Duquette and I went to Ottawa to obtain TLC charters. Needless to say, Percy Bengough was delighted to issue them.

Several weeks later we applied for certification. Although we had fulfilled the legal requirement of signing up a majority of the employees, the Labour Department ordered a secret vote to determine their wishes. In every case more voted for the union than had actually joined. With the unions certified I assumed responsibility for drafting and then negotiating the agreements, while Duquette undertook the organization of other plants.

The negotiations were not easy. The managements were inexperienced in collective bargaining and feared the unknown consequences of their actions. Moreover, in most cases, the people with whom we were negotiating lacked full authority from their superiors to make concessions on basic issues beyond predetermined positions.

Issues on which the company and unions disagreed were submitted to government conciliation. When this failed to result in agreement, which was usually the case, then the differences were submitted to arbitration. The formation of an arbitration board involved the selection of an impartial chairman and the designation of one representative from the union and one from the company. Then a brief had to be prepared and presented substantiating the union's case. Witnesses were called and questioned, and there was a good deal of argument. Finally, when both the union and the employer had completed their cases, the board retired to deliberate on a decision.

Meantime, we just waited, sometimes a month, sometimes two, and often more. When a decision was finally rendered it was usually a compromise between the two positions. Most often the parties agreed to accept the board's decision and proceeded to sign a contract. But sometimes the decision was unacceptable and the union would go on strike. In Quebec, unlike other provinces, decisions of arbitration boards were not mandatory. Eventually, negotiations would be resumed, and invariably an agreement would finally be reached.

I became fully occupied with a myriad of bargaining responsibilities. The unreasonable anti-union attitude of some employers, the slow progress in reaching an agreement, and the endless discussions and months of waiting for decisions of arbitration boards were, to say the least, frustrating. It took me a long time to adjust and curb my impatience.

With the end of the war in 1945 most of the war production plants closed and the unions we had established simply folded up. Some of the former members found employment in the rapidly-expanding peacetime industries and kept in touch with us. Those who found jobs in unionized plants often became active in union affairs; others who got work in non-union plants helped organize them.

Between 1943 and 1955 our organizing staff in Quebec increased significantly and in this period we organized 45 federal unions with a combined membership of over 10,000.

A most remarkable member of our staff in Quebec at the time was Phil Cutler.

I had met him at meetings of the Montreal Trades and Labour Council in the early 1940s. He was about four years younger than I, but he had considerable experience in the trade union movement. First, an officer in his own union, the Plumbers, he soon became the regional director for the AFL and he was involved in several crucial industrial disputes, notably with the Aluminum Company of Canada at Arvida. He was fluent in both English and French and had a graphic style in describing events. We soon gravitated to each other, both young, idealistic, and somewhat romantic about such virtues as human rights and justice.

In the post-war years we co-operated in various campaigns, supported or opposed the same issues. He joined the staff of the TLC in 1948, and, together with our families we became lifelong friends. The circumstances under which he joined the TLC staff were unusual, and demonstrated his character.

Shortly after the end of World War II, the American-based Seafarer's International Union moved to take over the jurisdiction of the Canadian Seamen's Union, an affiliate of the TLC. The AFL insisted that the SIU be admitted to the TLC.

The TLC Executive Council rejected the demand on the ground that the CSU already represented most of the merchant seamen in Canada. A number of officers of international unions which supported the AFL's position brought the dispute up at the 1948 TLC Convention in Victoria. After a lengthy and rather acrimonious debate, there was a roll-call vote, each delegate having to voice his or her support of opposition to the proposal. Cutler was a delegate and when his turn came he supported the TLC, even though he was employed by the AFL. A few weeks after the convention he was fired and Percy Bengough promptly engaged him as a member of the TLC staff.

About a year later he began studying for a degree in law. Although he had many responsibilities in his work, as well as some personal difficulties, he succeeded in getting a Bachelor of Arts degree from the University of Ottawa, and then his law degree from the University of Montreal. He began to practice law in 1954, specializing in labour law. In 1962 he undertook post-graduate studies at the University of Montreal, and received his diploma d'Études Supérieures in 1964 and his doctorate in law in 1968. Twenty years later he was named Judge of the Supreme Court of Quebec.

In the many years we have been colleagues and friends, I have always respected and admired his dedication and his indomitable spirit. He had served both the labour movement and the legal profession with great distinction.

CHAPTER FOUR
Organizing in Quebec

ALTHOUGH I LIVED IN QUEBEC almost ten years before I became a full-time union organizer, I had only a rudimentary knowledge of the French language. But in the early 1940s and 1950s, this was not a great problem for me. At that time English Canadians generally who could not speak French got along quite well, but French-Canadians who could not speak English had scant chance of filling key positions in either industry or unions.

When I spoke to workers in English, they seemed to understand what I was saying. And if some did not understand there was always someone who would give a French version of my message. In those years most union meetings and conferences were conducted in both English and French, but most of the discussions were in English.

The industries that I was trying to organize were in the main war munitions plants in Valleyfield and Boucherville, rubber plants in St. Jérôme, Lachine, and Grenby, mining industries in Murdochville and Thurso, brick manufacturing in Delson, meat packing in Montreal, textile plants in St. Jérôme and Lachute, and aluminum and paper containers in Montreal. In these industries most of management people at all levels were English who either lived in Quebec or who were brought to Quebec from other provinces or countries. Wherever I went in the province, in every industry in which I negotiated, with every government labour conciliator, and before every government appointed arbitration board to which I presented a brief or memorandum, English was the *de facto* language.

As collective agreements were negotiated in English, the company sometimes undertook to provide a French translation and in at least in one agreement to my knowledge (Dominion Rubber Co. in St. Jérôme) it was stipulated that if there appeared to be a discrepancy between the two version of the agreement, the English would be considered to be the official version.

In this case the union negotiating committee consisted of 12 men, and only two of them spoke English. The two who did not speak French were the plant manager, who came from Ontario, and I. The Company personnel officer, who was English with a good knowledge of French, provided the step-by-step translation.

Language certainly proved no impediment to my organizing efforts during World War II.

THE STRUGGLES AT ST. JÉROME

IN THE EARLY 1940s St. Jérôme, Quebec, was a community dominated by a small industrial power elite who controlled jobs, determined wages, and affected all aspects of their citizens' lives. Three companies were involved: Dominion Rubber Company, Rolland Paper Company, and Regent Knitting Mill. For a long time there were no unions in these companies, and when unions did become established, they had great difficulty effecting improvements and getting better working conditions.

The union at the Rolland Paper Mill had the advantage of being part of a strong organization that bargained for all intents and purposes on an industry-wide basis. Our union at Dominion Rubber had a slight advantage in the fact that the large rubber plants in Ontario negotiated with the much stronger international union, the United Rubber, Cork, Linoleum and Plastic Workers of America, which set a pattern for Quebec. But our local union at the Regent Knitting Mill (Local 254) had none of these advantages. Moreover, working conditions in the textile industry in Quebec, and in the country generally, were considerably below those in most other industries. The workers in these plants, however, were by no means docile or subservient to the companies. They fought hard to establish their unions, and then they fought just as hard to win decent wages and working conditions.

Negotiating the first agreement at the Regent Mill was an excruciatingly frustrating experience. The employer was Hyman Grower, who established himself as a one-man negotiating team on the company side. After a good deal of bargaining he would finally agree on a certain condition, and then, at the very next session, he would unashamedly announce that he had changed his mind, or that he had "been advised" not to accept what he had previously agreed to. Worse still, he would sometimes blatantly lie, saying he had not agreed to the condition.

I soon changed the procedure by having each clause of the proposed contract typed on a separate sheet. As a clause was negotiated, with whatever changes were agreed to, I asked Grower and our union president to sign the sheet "to avoid misunderstanding or misinterpretation of what has been agreed to." It seemed to work well, but from then on Grower brought his lawyer to the bargaining sessions.

The negotiations proceeded at a snail's pace, and it became apparent that we would have to submit our demands to arbitration. After several months the arbitration board gave a decision which, once again, was a compromise. Nevertheless, we were willing to accept it, but the company was not. And so, in the winter of 1945, we went on strike.

There were no scabs or strike-breakers. In St. Jérôme no worker would think of scabbing. We maintained an impressive picket line, but because of the terrible cold we had to change pickets every hour. At the union hall a group of workers' wives brewed coffee and made sandwiches. Local grocery stores contributed food and some citizens gave money to help the strikers.

There was at least one amusing incident. On the picket line some of the strikers, suffering from the cold, asked if it might be possible to have a bit of whiskey — "just to warm up." I told them I did not mind buying a few bottles, but it would not be a good idea to drink on the picket line because the community might get the idea that we were "boozing it up." I said I would buy two or three bottles that could be drunk in the union hall. I told them it was important that we not leave ourselves open to criticism, and they said they saw the logic of this, but they still wanted a drink.

Then I had an idea. I telephoned the Chief of Police, whom I had got to know quite well. I told him that the pickets wanted to spike their coffee with a little bit of whiskey because of the severe cold. In order to avoid false rumours, I would like him to assign officers as witnesses. He though the idea had merit, but said he could not assign an officer to be a witness to whiskey drinking.

"Of course not," I said, "but you could assign them to observe proper behaviour of the pickets, could you not?"

"Yes, I could do that," he responded.

"Good," I said. "Could you have them over in half an hour?"

He agreed. I rushed to the liquor store, bought two bottles of rye and returned to the union hall where I gave them to the picket captain, telling him "no more than two ounces in every cup." The policeman watched with broad smiles as he supervised "proper behaviour." The picket captain had a most peculiar idea of measurement, but who cared? Soon the cold grim faces of the pickets melted into smiles. Some began to sing, including my favourite French song, "Alouette."

In the two days that the worst of the cold lasted we bought five bottles, but there was not a ripple of objection in the community. Only the pickets and the police knew about it. Obviously, I had been unnecessarily concerned about our image, not knowing well enough the earthiness of the St. Jérôme workers.

The strike lasted for two bitterly cold weeks, and then the company called me to resume negotiations.

"To negotiate what?" I asked Grower.

"To negotiate the report of the arbitration board," he replied.

"The board did not make a report," I explained. "The board rendered a judgment and it is not negotiable. We have already said that we are willing to accept it. Now the ball is in your court. You either accept that decision as it is, or we stay out."

The following day the company lawyer telephoned to say that Grower was ready to accept the board's decision. We met, and in due course an agreement was signed. However, labour-management relations at the Regent Mill were never good. They remained strained, and I avoided participating in subsequent negotiations or other dealings with the company, assigning Victor Trudeau, a TLC organizer and a tough negotiator.

ST. JÉROME POSTSCRIPT

IN ST. JÉROME the Catholic Church openly and strongly supported the workers in their struggles, mainly through the efforts of a highly-admired and respected parish priest, Monsignor Dubois. When I first met him, he was already more than 70 years of age. He was of slight build with thin light hair and watery blue eyes. He spoke slowly in a low voice with measured words, as if he were searching for the right English expression.

When the workers were organizing, he had often encouraged them from the pulpit. A few months before I went to St. Jérôme there had been a strike and Monsignor Dubois made the church basement available to be used as the strike headquarters. In other similar situations the workers always knew that their parish priest would support, encourage, and give them solace in their troubles.

I was introduced to him by Paul Dalpe, who knew him well. The circumstances under which we met arose from a serious threat to jobs in the Dominion Rubber factory. Shortly after the war, Japan, getting back on its industrial feet, began to export rubber footwear to Canada in large quantities. India and Czechoslovakia were also exporting footwear to Canada and Dominion Rubber at St. Jérôme began eliminating some lines of production and laying off workers. When we raised the matter with the company they said, with honesty and frankness, that they could not possibly compete with the Japanese imports, and they showed us the figures.

The manufacture of rubber footwear was extremely labour-intensive, and because the cost of production in Japan and other countries was so much lower than in Canada, the company said it had no alternative to cutting the volume of its output. Worse, the future of even the curtailed production was highly uncertain. We asked why Japan and other countries were allowed to flood the Canadian market, when there was no need for such imports. We were told it was government policy. I asked why the company had not asked the government to apply reasonable restrictions. The company said the entire footwear industry had petitioned the federal government, but no action had been taken. When I asked why the union had not been asked to join in the petition, there was no answer.

Something had to be done to safeguard the jobs of our members. We held a special meeting of the Executive Committee and someone asked why the union could not go to the government and explain our serious concern, not only for the rubber workers, but for the whole community. We all knew that if Dominion closed it would be catastrophic to the area. And so, through the TLC, I arranged a meeting with officials for the Department of Trade and Commerce, which was headed by the Hon. C.D. Howe, a senior member of the Cabinet. We selected three Executive Board members to go with me and, although it was mid-winter, we decided to hire a taxi in order to go to Ottawa and return the same day. None of us owned a car.

A few days before we were to leave it occurred to me that it would strengthen our case if some well-known and respected citizen joined our delegation to express the concern of the community as a whole. I discussed the idea with Dalpe who said he knew such a person, but he was elderly and might not want to drive all the way to Ottawa and back in such unpredictable weather. The person he had in mind was the parish priest, Monsignor Dubois. He telephoned the Monsignor and we went immediately to see him. I found him very easy to talk to. After we explained the situation concerning imports and the adverse effect on the workers we told him our plans and asked if he would be willing to join us. There was no hesitation or detailed questioning. He just asked when we were going and said he would be ready to be picked up.

Two days later, at seven o'clock in the morning, he was waiting, all bundled up. The narrow road from St. Jérôme to Ottawa turned and twisted in all directions. As luck would have it we had a slight accident when another car slid into our taxi. Despite the wind and cold we all got out to inspect the damage, including the Monsignor. After an exchange of information we continued on our way. The damage had ben slight, but much to our regret and discomfort, the car heater had ceased to function. We continued, chilled to the bone. I noticed the Monsignor was a little shaken by the accident, but he made no complaint nor reference to it.

We finally arrived in Ottawa, a little late for our meeting, and found several officials waiting. I introduced myself and the other union officers. Monsignor Dubois was slowly unwrapping himself and I introduced him as "the distinguished representative of the St. Jérôme community." To our surprise we were told that the

Minister would be joining the meeting, but only for a few minutes because of other commitments. He arrived and as he shook hands with me explained: "Sorry I'm late. I'm busy building a pipeline you know." His small, sharp, gray eyes sparkled.

He said that, although he could not stay to hear all our story, he knew why we had come. Often the government faced a dilemma and had to cope as best it could, he said. He apologized, shook hands again, and left. Then it was our turn. First I outlined our concerns and specifically requested some form of quota on the importation of rubber footwear. Paul Dalpe also spoke; and then the Monsignor said he would like to add "just an opinion."

He began by describing the community of St. Jérôme — the absence of serious crime, the extent of the educational facilities, the number of churches. It was a vivid picture of the little community in the Laurentians.

"Why do we have a stable and happy community?" he asked. "Because most of our people have jobs. If our people are laid off there are very few jobs outside our three main industries. What happens to them? Where will they go? What will become of them?"

He pointed at us, "The union cannot give them jobs."

He pointed to himself,"The Church cannot give them jobs. But they are not asking for jobs, most of them have jobs today. What we are all asking for is that these jobs that my people have will be safeguarded."

It was a moving speech. He touched us all very deeply with his simple but expressive sentiment. We received the usual government response — appreciation for our visit, assurance that there was now a better understanding of the situation, and a commitment that the Minister would do all in his power to meet our request, at least partially.

The meeting had lasted almost two hours. When it was over we all bundled back into the taxi and began our journey back to St. Jérôme. It was dark when we arrived and drove the Monsignor to his home. We all got out to shake his hand and thank him most sincerely for joining us and making such an effective speech. In his humble way he thanked us, thinking it might be of some help. Then, just before he entered the doorway, he turned, and speaking French said: "I'll see you all in church on Sunday."

The government never did take any steps whatsoever to curb the importations, and as a result more and more of the workers at St. Jérôme were laid off. In a few years production stopped completely.

BACK TO THE 18TH CENTURY

THE CANADIAN REFRACTORIES MINE at Kilmar, Quebec, some 30 miles north-east of Montreal, produced magnesite, which was used in the manufacture of brick used for lining blast furnaces in steel mills and similar operations.

When I first visited Kilmar, I was shocked at the living and working conditions of the miners. Dust from the mine covered the entire community, making it a desolate white area with not a tree or a blade of grass. The miners' homes were small, crudely-constructed log cabins without water or sanitary facilities. The single men lived in bunkhouses under similar conditions. I talked to one man,

Lucien Tremblay, who later became vice-president of our union. He told me he had lived in Kilmar for 30 years, and had never had a bathroom in his house.

In the process of organizing the workers into the Federal Local 245 I made an appointment to see the plant manager, Norman Pitt. He was a tall slender Englishman with a thin pointed face, small gray eyes, and a mouth that seemed never to have smiled. I remember our conversation well.

"Mr. Pitt, I very much appreciate meeting with you. As you are no doubt aware the Trades and Labour Congress is organizing the workers in your company, and we hope that, in due course, we can establish good relations with you," I opened.

He replied, "Mr. Swerdlow, first I have difficulty pronouncing your name. Secondly, I didn't want to refuse to see you because I didn't know exactly what you wanted to see me about. Thirdly, I can't stop you from organizing my employees, but I certainly have no intention of negotiating a union agreement with you or anyone else. Now, if you would be good enough, I am busy, that is all the time I can give you."

I said, "Very well," and left the office. I then convened a meeting of the workers and related the conversation with their manager. They were furious, and then and there voted to strike. The following day I telephoned the company from Montreal and told the person who answered the telephone that as of a certain date the workers would strike. The strike took place as scheduled and lasted about three hours. Then Pitt telephoned me, and our conversation went along these lines:

"Hello Mr. Swerdlow, how are you today? I guess there must have been some misunderstanding between us. It seems you reported to your union that I would not negotiate with you."

"That is correct Mr. Pitt, that is exactly what you said to me."

"I think, Mr. Swerdlow, you took me too literally. Why don't you come over to the plant and we can talk this thing over."

"I would be more than happy to do that, Mr. Pitt."

Shortly after, Canadian Refractories recognized our union and negotiated an agreement with us. Moreover, Pitt became a good friend of the TLC. Our relationship thereafter was as good as one could expect. But something should be said about the first agreement I negotiated with the company. It contained some unique provisions, such as: "The company undertakes to install running water and toilet facilities in the homes of the workers at the earliest possible date. The company will also provide, at once, adequate sheets and blankets for the needs of the bunkhouse."

This clearly indicated the living conditions that prevailed in the mid-twentieth century at Kilmar, before the union arrived.

MEN AND MACHINES

THE CANADIAN IMPORT COMPANY, a branch of the Dominion Steel and Coal Corporation, was located at the Port of Montreal, engaged in unloading coal from ships. Specifically, a crew of 18 men would go down each hold and shovel coal to the opening so that it could be removed. Our local, Federal Union 102, was small in numbers but strong in organization. The members took their union very seriously.

One day the company announced that it was bringing in "mechanical trimmers." These were small tractors that were lowered in to move the coal, thus replacing the 18 men. Our collective agreement clearly stated that each gang should consist of 18 men; consequently, reducing the size of the gang was contrary to the agreement. The company agreed with us on this point and the six mechanical trimmers were put in storage on the company's property. In the four months remaining for the agreement the workers walking by looked at the trimmers, wondering if and when they would lose their jobs, replaced by machines.

We knew, of course, that once the agreement expired the company intended bringing in the machines and laying off men. I also knew that the problem could not be solved by discussion with the management. We would have to go to arbitration, and we did. This was at a period in which a number of companies were introducing some form of higher technology or "automation," as it was loosely described. I thought a great deal about the presentation we would make to the arbitration board. The introduction of new forms of mechanization is usually done in the name of "progress," but I have always equated progress in terms of human values and human welfare. I decided to approach the problem on that ground. When the arbitration board was finally set up the parties agreed upon Judge Charles Gurin as chairman. I knew him to be a fine, warm human being and a devout Catholic.

I went to see Father O'Connell at the Thomas More Institute in Montreal to ask for his assistance in preparing a case on humane grounds. He suggested I should read the encyclical entitled "Rerum Novarum." I found a great deal of common sense and fairness in the encyclical and quoted from it at length in my presentation. Finally the company's lawyer, Tommy Carr, interrupted, saying: "Mr. Chairman, I protest Mr. Swerdlow coming here as if he were speaking from the pulpit, and quoting a lot of...." He was searching for the appropriate word, and I am afraid I put it in his mouth when I suggested: "A lot of junk."

"Yes, a great deal of junk," he blurted out. Judge Gurin looked at him, and then after making a note on his papers, asked me to continue.

The outcome of the case was that the board ruled: (1) None of the workers were to be laid off because of the introduction of the machines; (2) If a worker quit or retired, a new worked did not necessarily have to be engaged; (3) There should be no forced early retirement; in other words, the company could introduce the mechanical trimmers, but not at the expense of laid-off workers. The company accepted the decision.

This was the first such arbitration case in the Province of Quebec.

THE CASE OF THE SLIDE RULE

AN UNUSUAL SITUATION involving the use of a slide rule occurred at the British Rubber Company at Lachine, Quebec. The company, which was established shortly after World War II, manufactured rubber footwear. We began to organize the plant before it was fully operational, and after a comparatively short campaign we succeeded in signing up a majority of the employees and obtaining certification. In due course we opened negotiations, which were in the main patterned after the collective agreement at the Dominion Rubber Company at St. Jérôme.

However, because the company had begun to manufacture only six or seven months before the union was established, a proper wage pattern had not been established. In the rubber footwear industry throughout Canada most workers were on some form of job evaluation. As soon as our negotiations began, the company engaged an industrial engineer to introduce what they called "a universally accepted scientific job evaluation system."

The engineer employed was Claude Marion, who, we were told, was highly experienced and trained in introducing, developing, and refining job evaluation systems to determine wage rates. But, when the time came to consider and analyze the many, many jobs in the plant, trying to relate the value of one job to another, we ran into considerable difficulties with the company.

The introduction of job evaluation in any plant is not an easy operation. It involves a great deal of minute detail in the comparison of different jobs. There is a great deal of stopwatch timing and lengthy discussion as to which worker is to be used as a criteria to establish the time required for a particular operation. It is a highly complicated procedure.

When I first met Marion, he seemed a very pleasant, low-profile person. He did not appear overly set in his opinions. He looked like, and obviously was, a scholarly person who knew his function. He had been employed by the company to perform certain duties in a specified time. The union executive had to meet with him frequently to discuss each and every job, and to try to agree on a formula establishing a minimum rate, and then the escalation of reward based on the quality and quantity of production. In establishing a formula, industrial engineers, by their very nature, rely on the answers they get from their slide rule. Marion had a very impressive rule, more than a foot in length, which he carried continually, using it at every opportunity.

The agreement specified two objectives with regard to job evaluation: it had to be fair, and it had to be understood by the workers so they would know exactly what they were earning, based on quantity and quality of their work. Of course, none of the union officers understood the mysteries of the slide rule. Thus, when Marion used his rule to substantiate a point, it had little meaning to them. He would show a union officer the answer on his instrument, but it had no meaning and atmosphere of distrust quickly developed between the officers and the engineer. Their relationship deteriorated.

Finally, Marion called my officer and said he had a problem.

"I don't seem to be able to get along with your union boys, and I don't know the reason," he said. "Believe me, Mr. Swerdlow, I am leaning over backward to introduce the kind of system that will give the workers everything they are entitled to, but I just don't seem to be able to win the confidence of the union boys."

I told him our people were reasonable and intelligent and that there must be something I didn't know about. Marion said it was essential that they get along together if an equitable wage system were to be developed. I said I would try to find out what the difficulty was.

Several days later I met with the president of the local, Marcel Ouelette, and asked him how they were getting along with Marion.

"We are not getting along," he said.

"Why not?" I asked.

"We can't speak to that guy."

"Why not?"

"You know, brother Max, every time we speak to that guy and raise an issue or a problem, he doesn't talk back to you. You know what he does? He pulls out his slide rule and pushes it one way and pulls it another, and then he says: 'There is the answer.' You can't dispute that. I look at the slide rule, but I don't know what he is talking about. Every time you talk to Marion all his answers are on the slide rule."

I went to Marion and told him what I thought. He seemed to feel I had a point and asked what he should do. I suggested he teach the president of the local, and perhaps the secretary, how to read a slide rule, which should be possible to do in a few days, or at the most a week. He said he would. I didn't hear anything further for several weeks and then there were some discussions with the company in which I was involved. With considerable inner amusement I noticed the president of the local had a slide rule sticking out of his overall pocket and, from time to time, he would use it to ascertain a figure. It was not a subject of conversation, but I did ask both the president and Marion how they were getting along, and they both said the situation had improved considerably.

When Marion completed his work his contract with the company terminated. Shortly after, when the union and the company reached an impasse on a number of job classifications, which became subject to arbitration, the union engaged him to prepare and present our case. As I listened to the proceedings my thoughts drifted back to Marion's mystic slide rule, and I was amused at the turn of events.

THE MISSING TABLEWARE

SHORTLY, AFTER THE SIGNING of the first agreement at Defence Industries Limited at Verdun, I met with the senior supervisor of personnel to discuss a number of in-plant matters, such as establishing a union office on the premises, union bulletin boards, and so on. When we neared the end of the meeting the supervisor, Eric Taylor, told me the company had a difficult problem and needed the full co-operation of the union to find a solution.

"What is the problem?" I asked.

"Well," he said, "someone in the plant is stealing tableware from the cafeteria."

I was not sure I had heard him correctly,.

He continued very seriously: "Yes," he repeated. "Tableware has been vanishing mysteriously, and in increasing numbers."

I still thought he was joking and said: "Come on Eric, why make such a fuss over a few missing spoons."

He almost jumped out of his chair, bellowing: "Just a couple of spoons? Let me tell you what a couple consists of."

He took a typewritten sheet from his desk drawer and holding it up said it was an article to be printed in the company's monthly publication, "Silver Bulletin." I read:

Within a year 14,640 or more table articles have been taken. This enormous figure breaks down in to 7,200 teaspoons, 2,400 knives, 2,800 forks and 2,160 soup spoons. Recently 600 teaspoons were brought in on a Monday, by Wednesday night 219 were missing. This is an important matter around DIL these days, for if the supply of tableware continues to disappear, there looms the prospect of each employee having to bring his own eating equipment.

I must admit I was impressed with someone's enterprise, but I asked in what way the union could co-operate in solving the problem.

"Just tell your boys to keep their eyes open and report to me personally anyone seen taking the tableware," he replied.

"No Eric," I said. "The union can't be policeman for the company."

"Of course not, but your boys can co-operate, can't they?"

"That kind of co-operation means fingering someone and that is not our job," I answered. "You better solve the problem yourself."

The discussion ended on that note and I heard nothing more about the case. It seemed to me someone must have been taking the cutlery and selling it, an ingenious way to make an extra buck.

HELPING COMPANY COMMUNICATIONS

WITH SOME 45 LOCALS to service, we were very much involved in settling grievances, most of which were related to conditions clearly outlined in the agreement. One such occasion occurred at the Dominion Tar and Chemical Company at Delson, Quebec. There the company produced a variety of chemicals. The workers were represented by Federal Local 174.

In the plant there was a designated area where highly inflammable chemicals were stored and smoking was strictly prohibited. On this occasion a worker who had 15 years service went there to get some material, and, without thinking, lit a cigarette. A foreman arrived and saw him smoking. The employee was immediately ordered out of the section and told not to bother going to the head office but to go home. The following day the man returned to the plant to report for work and was told he had been fired. He protested, and the local union president took the grievance to the plant manager, asking the reason for his discharge. The manager carefully explained the danger of smoking in that area and pointed out that there were "No Smoking" signs all over the place. Furthermore, our agreement specifically stated that smoking in prohibited areas was a cause for reprimand or dismissal.

The union president telephoned me and told me what had happened. "Well, what can be done?" I asked. "Obviously he was wrong. He should have known better, but let me think about it. Maybe I can come up with a solution, but clearly we don't have a case."

I thought about it a great deal, and finally decided I should talk, not with the plant manager, who was just doing his job, but with the president of the company, a Mr. Prudhomme, at the head office in Montreal. I arranged an appointment and when we met he impressed me as being a very sensible and kind man. However, he saw no excuse for the employee, who, he said, should have known better than violating such an important rule.

I asked him just how important it was that there should be no smoking in that area, and I must say he gave me an explanation that I had not realized. He told me that within a combined area there was dust which, if ignited, could cause a very serious explosion. Moreover, and this was a point he emphasized, the plant was heavily insured against fires and explosions, and if the insurance company learned that an employee was caught smoking in a prohibited area was not reprimanded, the insurance could either be cancelled or the premiums raised significantly. I could not counteract that argument, but as he was talking, a thought crossed my mind.

"Mr. Prudhomme, to what extent are the workers aware of the real danger of smoking in prohibited areas?" I asked.

"The insurance company insists on many visible signs and we have complied with that condition," he said. "The signs are in both French and English, 'No Smoking Allowed.'"

"Yes, of course," I said, "but that does not necessarily mean that if one violated the restriction he is, in fact, endangering his own life and the lives of others, as well as the property."

"I suppose that is right," Prudhomme agreed.

"Mr. Prudhomme," I went on, "you are quite within your rights in dismissing this worker, I am not disputing that. However, how sure are you that another workers won't do the same thing? How sure are you that the workers really understand the danger of smoking in the prohibited areas? The fact that you have signs on the wall does not necessarily emphasize the seriousness and possible consequence of smoking there. Don't you think the whole cause of safety would be better served if, in addition to the signs, which may be meaningless, you took the time to explain why the signs are there and what might happen if they are ignored? Why don't you explain to them so they can understand the danger of lighting a match in an area filled with explosive dust?

He pondered the question, then replied: "Well you're right. We haven't really conveyed to the workers the seriousness and the danger, but there is nothing I can do about the chap who was fired. The plant manager fired him and I'm not going over his head. What do you think the plant manager would look like if, as a result of you and I meeting, I was to overrule his decision?"

"That's the last thing I would want you to do, Mr. Prudhomme."

"Mr. Swerdlow," he asked, a bit impatiently, "what are you asking me to do?"

"First," I said, "I recommend that very soon you ask the plant manger to convene a meeting of all your employees — there are about 120 of them. Get them together, refer to the worker who was fired for smoking and explain exactly why he was fired. It would not be sufficient merely to point to the agreement and say 'He violated the contract.' You should point out why that condition is in the agreement in the first place — the real danger of smoking. You have to make an impact on the employees so that, even if they have an opportunity without a foreman watching, they will not, for their own safety. Then, if your insurance company is so set on the regulations, it might be a good idea to have a representative of the insurance company there to substantiate what you are doing. Next, it seems to me that the plant manager who dismissed the employee might in a week or two, or even three, call him back, after you have this meeting with the employees. The man could be told that because of his long years of service, and because there are no other industries in Delson where he might find work, he will be given another chance. The result will be that you have accomplished your objective in impressing the workers, and the plant manager will be regarded as a good and pretty generous guy. In a small community like Delson that is an important consideration."

Prudhomme was obviously impressed, he said he thought my ideas had merit. The dismissal of the employee was, after all, intended to warn the others, and he thought the idea of explaining the seriousness of the situation was sound. He said he would think about it and telephone me in a few days.

Before leaving his office I thought there was one other point I should make.

"Mr. Prudhomme," I said, "my discussion with you is obviously not a condition that would allow us to go through the normal grievance procedure, arbitration or what have you. I am not suggesting for a moment that I will go back to the local and tell the president and the executive that I have met with you. I am not interested in winning a grievance. I am interested in one thing only — I would like to see the worker re-employed, and I would like to see safety assured. I am not seeking a minor victory; I am seeking a solution. If the situation is resolved, more or less along the lines I have suggested, the union will be satisfied, and so will you."

We shook hands, he thanked me and I left. A few days later he telephoned and told me he had spoken to the plant manager and to the insurance company. The whole situation had been discussed with the employees, who were clearly impressed. At the same time he had informed the workers that the dismissal of the individual would be reconsidered. About a week later the man was called in and offered his job back, on condition that he never again violate the regulations.

I never told the president or officers of the local of my meeting with Prudhomme. It was not important that they know. I was quite content that the worker was re-employed. After all, that was the important thing, wasn't it?

LOVE IN THE STOREROOM

ON ONE OCCASION an absolutely unique incident took place at the Lachine plant of British Rubber. In all my experiences in settling grievances, and in conciliation and arbitration cases, this was the only time I was ever confronted with such circumstances. The case involved a young man and woman who were found by their supervisor in a storeroom in the process of making love. Naturally it was a very embarrassing situation for them, as well as for the supervisor. The matter was reported to the assistant manager, Gerry Dolan, who telephoned asking me to come to the plant as quickly as possible. When I enquired what the problem was he gave a sketchy explanation and said he intended dismissing the employees, but wanted to discuss it with me first.

At the plant he related what he had been told by the supervisor. I accepted the story, having no reason to believe it to be false. However, when Dolan said he was going to dismiss the employees, I asked on what ground.

"On the ground of making love," he replied.

"Gerry," I said, "the conditions of dismissal are embodied in the collective agreement, and there is nothing there that says lovemaking is a cause for dismissal."

"How could a collective agreement embody such a condition?" he asked.

"I'm not suggesting it should," I went on, "but the fact remains that dismissing an employee is serious business, and that is why the agreement specifies the conditions for which an employee may be dismissed — and lovemaking is not one of the conditions."

He had become impatient and somewhat agitated.

"Max, you can't sit there and tell me that when a man and a woman go into the storeroom and make love that is all right and they should not be reprimanded."

"Perhaps some form of discipline might be taken," I suggested, "but I could not support, and in fact would fight like hell against the dismissal of these two employees. After all, Gerry, are you so set against making love? What objection do you have?"

"Max," he said, "I have nothing against lovemaking, but I object to lovemaking on company time and on company property."

I laughed, and after a moment he joined in. When he cooled down we tried to discuss the matter in a more serious vein. I said I thought the idea of dismissal should be forgotten. We searched for another means to discipline the employees and finally found it in the agreement. They should have a mild reprimand for "leaving the place of work without permission." This was written into the contract as grounds for disciplinary action.

Well, in all the years I had been involved in the settlement of grievances I had never experienced such a situation.

CHAPTER FIVE
The Quebec Labour Movement:
Some Leaders and Some Internal Battles

THE SIZE OF THE LABOUR MOVEMENT today often disguises its relatively tiny roots in the decades of my earliest activity. For example, when I first visited Percy Bengough at the Ottawa headquarters of the TLC, the office consisted of only the chief himself as full-time President, a part-time secretary-treasurer (Arthur Daoust), an office manager (Arthur Hemming), and two stenographers, one of whom was Bengough's private secretary. I became the TLC's first full-time organizer, although Carl Berg in Edmonton was occasionally on the payroll as a western organizer. In the early 1950s Leslie Wismer was added to the staff.

The small size of the movement made many of its leaders seem larger than life and this was particularly true in Quebec. Some of the personalities who stand out in my memory are worthy of further description.

RAOUL TREPANIER

WHEN I FIRST BEGAN ATTENDING meetings of the Montreal Trades and Labour Council the chairman was Raoul Trepanier, a member of the Amalgamated Association of Street Railway, Electric, and Motor Coach Employees. I was very impressed with him. A heavily built man of medium height, he had a short, thick neck, a full mouth, and blue-gray eyes. He conducted the meetings with authority, dignity, and formality. Whether he was presiding or mingling with the delegates, he looked massive, solid, and strong. He spoke clearly and slowly with a deep voice. He was a man of balanced temperament and never ruffled.

I learned a great deal from him. However heated the discussion might become, he summarized the differences succinctly and factually, and then asked the delegates to vote. He always liked to maintain as much harmony as possible, even when the debate became particularly hostile.

He knew parliamentary procedure well and applied the rules fairly but firmly, being quick to interrupt any speaker who tried to circumvent the rules. His attitude toward new or younger delegates was more flexible. He took the position that young delegates, lacking experience, should be given a chance to learn, and the council was a good place for that.

My colleague, Adrienne Villeneuve, has described Raoul Trepanier in these words:

He impressed me so much that, in fact, he became my teacher, without my knowing it. I followed him for many years, analyzing and admiring the way he handled the difficult issues that were being debated. He had a sharp analytical mind. He was a master at identifying and separating the most salient features in a given situation and in putting the question to the delegates. Generally he was supported by the Council.

I never knew Raoul Trepanier to support or be aligned with any particular group in the Council. I never heard him embarrass or humiliate a delegate when he was speaking. I never heard him say anything derogatory about anyone. It seemed to me that he was a man without prejudice or malice.

ARTHUR MARTEL

ARTHUR MARTEL, the Canadian Vice-President of the United Brotherhood of Carpenters and Joiners of America, was also a remarkable man. I knew him well, but there was one aspect that I did not know until Adrienne Villeneuve told me:

If there was ever a self-made man, it was Arthur Martel. He could neither read nor write. I knew him well and often travelled with him. Sometimes he asked me to read his ticket or his mail. He never had a pencil and paper, and never took notes. He just reclined in his chair, usually with his eyes closed, and listened. He had a computerized mind and retained details of discussion.

Arthur Martel was a colourful personality. He was of average height, with a roguish lined face, with small eyes that were always sharp, but at the same time provocative and mischievous. He dressed casually and always looked like a typical worker. The exception, and one that seemed a contradiction of his personality, was an impressive diamond ring which he wore. He spoke both French and English fluently. His humour was never flippant; it was direct, pointed, and always had meaning.

I recall that he once stood for office in the Quebec Federation of Labour. Though he was respected and highly regarded by most of those who knew him, he was never elected to any important position except that of Vice-President of his own union. At that convention he was defeated, and after the vote the candidates were offered the opportunity of going to the platform to make a statement. Arthur Martel walked slowly to the front. From the platform he looked at the audience for a minute, and then, in perfect English, he said: "Friends, you have made your choice, that is good enough for me. I know that you have made a serious mistake. May God have mercy on your souls."

Ideologically and philosophically he was conservative. On one occasion, when a Quebec Federation of Labour convention was discussing legislation to provide more paid holidays, he spoke passionately against the resolution on these grounds.

If the government is going to enact this kind of legislation, then you will ask them to enact more legislation, and soon you will be completely relying on the government to improve working conditions for our members. At that point, my friends, collective bargaining will be meaningless.

While he had some support, the resolution was accepted by a large majority of the delegates. His conservative attitude was out of line with the younger trade unionists. He lived in the past, could not understand the present, nor see the future.

Arthur Martel remained active to the age of 80 and died when he was 85.

ALPHAGE BODOIN

THE FUTURE OF THE TRADE UNION MOVEMENT was being fashioned by younger trade unionists, one of whom was Alphage Bodoin of the Amalgamated Association of Street Railway, Electric, and Motor Coach Employees. He eventually became president of the Quebec Federation of Labour.

Alphage Bodoin was a man of mystery; little was known about him. He was neither admired nor disliked, and he had few personal friends, although I considered myself one of them. He was a man of average height, slightly built, and might be regarded as handsome. By nature he was very serious and gave the impression of never being very happy. When he occasionally smiled, it seemed to be an effort. He had a phobia about germs and microbes and tried to avoid touching things with his bare hands. He dressed immaculately and never appeared untidy or unshaven. He loved big cars and his proudest possession was his own, which he described as his living room and bedroom.

He was very positive in his approaches. For instance, once when the Quebec Government was about to amend the Labour Code, and when delegates to a convention were almost unanimously opposed to the revisions, Bodoin warned them:

> Our official position will be decided by your vote, there is no question about that. But, before you vote let's look at the positive aspects of these amendments, for I believe there are some provisions that are positive.

He went on to cite the sections which he considered not bad and warned that there was a danger of "throwing out the baby with the bath water." He took the position that, while the government should be made aware of the Federation's objections, it should also be told of the provisions which had labour's support.

Such was his attitude toward many contentious issues. He did not mind, from time to time, taking an unpopular position. He had a pragmatic approach and the courage to express his views, even if they were not popular. He was elected president of the Federation on the basis of his personal strength and unique personality. He never had a "political machine." Personally, I always supported him and campaigned for him, though he never asked me to, nor did he ever enquire about his chances of being elected.

ROGER PROVOST

AFTER THE DEATH OF ALPHAGE BODOIN, Roger Provost became president of the Quebec Federation of Labour. He had joined the labour movement as an organizer for the Millinery Workers' Union, Local 49, and then became a representative for the United Textile Workers of America. He was a man of average height, slim, and quite handsome. He was fluent in both French and English and had a charming, almost debonair, manner. He was popular and highly respected.

Adrienne Villeneuve described him thus:

Roger Provost was an intellectual. He spoke like a university professor, but if you looked at his hands, you would swear they were the hands of a plumber. His speeches were well constructed and articulately delivered. He had an extraordinarily well co-ordinated mind and a quick wit. Unlike Alphage Bodoin, when he lost an issue that was then; there was no vindictiveness in him.

At one point he was an unsuccessful candidate for the CCF in a general election. He died young, at the age of 42.

From the first time I first joined the labour movement, I was impressed with the leaders, people like Raoul Trepanier, Alphage Bodoin, Roger Provost, Claude Jodoin and others. All were dedicated men, committed to the labour movement, and, above all, they were good human beings.

The Quebec labour movement was, of course, even more divided than the English Canadian. In addition to the unfortunate battle between the TLC and CLC unions, there were also the Catholic unions to contend with. Nevertheless my two major experiences of union raiding involved TLC-CLC conflict.

UNION RAIDING

ONE OF THE QUEBEC INDUSTRIES in which we accomplished near total organization was meat packing. In all the other provinces the major meat packing plants were organized by the United Packinghouse Workers (CCL-CIO). In 1946 in Quebec we set up what we ambitiously called the National Council, composed of our meat packing locals in Quebec. In addition to other activities, we planned "inviting" the packinghouse workers in other provinces to leave the UPWA and join our National Council, thus becoming part of the Trades and Labour Congress rather than the Canadian Congress of Labour.

In fall 1946, I urged President Bengough to allow us to go to Edmonton to extend the "invitation" to workers in Canada Packers and Swift. He was not enthusiastic, calling it "a raiding venture," and somewhat sarcastically asking whether there were no unorganized workers in Quebec who needed a union. Obviously there were, I said, but not in the meat packing industry. I argued that so long as the meat packing unions in the TLC were confined to Quebec, we would be subject to the collective agreements negotiated by the much larger and more powerful UPWA. Sooner or later we would lose our locals to them, as it would be in their best interest to raid us. With some reluctance and obvious misgiving, Percy Bengough finally authorized me to go ahead.

I went to Edmonton with Rémi Duquette. We had been there only two or three weeks when President Bengough telephoned ordering us back to St. Jérôme post-haste: our Dominion Rubber Local 144 was being raided.

"By whom?" I asked. "By your friend Paul Fournier," he replied. I was shocked. Paul Fournier was a colleague who had often assisted me in organizing campaigns. Moreover, he was the assistant manager of my own union, the United Hatters. In addition he had, in some mysterious manner, become the Canadian representative of the Distillery Workers' International Union, which was also affiliated to the TLC. His Distillery Union had a collective agreement with Seagram's Distillery, and with a small local in the Dominion Rubber Company at Montreal, but he had at no time been given jurisdiction in the rubber industry. But this did not prevent Paul Fournier from claiming jurisdiction for the Dominion Rubber workers at St. Jérôme. The irony of the situation was that, while I was trying to raid a competing union from the other Congress, our union was being raided by one of our affiliates.

At St. Jérôme we found that the president and secretary of our local, as well as several members of the executive board, had joined the Distillery Workers and were trying to recruit others. We also learned that Fournier had been in St. Jérôme about two weeks, meeting with some of our officers and convincing them that their best interests would be served if the Montreal and St. Jérôme plants of Dominion Rubber were in the same union.

Those of our officers who had not joined him were confused and discouraged by these developments. They could not understand how or why one union, affiliated to a national labour federation, could raid another union, chartered by the same federation. They were waiting for guidance and leadership from us.

I telephoned President Bengough, bringing him up to date on the situation and explaining that I wanted to fight the Fournier raid, even if it meant a jurisdictional dispute with one of our affiliates.

"Hell," he said, "there will be no jurisdictional dispute between Paul Fournier and the Congress. That bloke has not and will not be given jurisdiction over rubber workers." Then he added a quip to the effect that "booze and rubber don't mix." I told him that, if we wanted to retain our local and recoup the loyalty of those who had resigned, two things were necessary: a carefully designed campaign that would progressively lead to that objective and the employment of a full-time business agent at St. Jérôme to head up the campaign. He pointed out that we already had two organizers in Montreal.

"Yes," I responded, "But in my opinion the situation requires someone on the scene all the time. Furthermore, if we should lose the Dominion Rubber local, we may also lose the Regent Knitting Mill local, but if we retain our rubber local, then our overall membership in St. Jérôme, together with groups a full-time business agent may organize, will more than justify the expenditure."

He hesitated and I was conscious of his uncertainty and reluctance to agree to another staff member. I rather expected him to say that he had not been elected to preside over the liquidation of the Congress treasury. I quickly added: "Chief, give me the ammunition and I'll finish the job." Finally, he simply said, "OK."

We called together a small group of our local's remaining officers and I told them of my conversation with the President of the Congress, and our determination to maintain our legal status as the bargaining agent because the Distillery Workers had no justifiable claim on the jurisdiction. Someone suggested a special emergency membership meeting. This was a step I would normally have supported, but on this occasion I was opposed. I reasoned that if we could be sure of a large attendance, it would enhance our position, on the other hand, if only a small number attended there could be a damaging reaction. The risk was too great, and, at the same time, calling such a meeting might give the impression that we were in a serious predicament.

Rather, I suggested our strategy should be to not treat the raid too seriously, but to regard it as little more than a flea bite. Since we were established as the legal bargaining agent with a contract that did not expire for another four months, we should continue to conduct our affairs as usual. We should appoint a president and secretary to act until an election for these posts could be held at a regular membership meeting. We should also appoint a business agent, preferably an employee of the plant. Finally, these actions and decisions should be conveyed to the membership. The group accepted these suggestions.

There were a number of proposals for the position of business agent, one of whom was Paul Émile Dalpe, a quality inspector at the plant. He was supported unanimously, and when I interviewed him the following day, I immediately realized that he was the man for the job. About 27 years of age, he had a reasonably good educational background and an agile mind, responding quickly and positively. He was an impressive speaker in both languages and was popular in the plant, having been active on behalf of the union in its efforts to organize the clerical employees, who were outside our local.

When I offered him the job, he indicated he was interested, but wanted to know how long it would last. I explained the situation and the likelihood of a Labour Board vote, and I continued:

"If we win the vote, you win the job. If we lost he vote...."

"Then I lose the job," he quickly interjected.

"That's right," I said.

He accepted the offer with enthusiasm and determination, regardless of the uncertainty of his continued employment.

A day or two after he joined our staff we issued an announcement criticizing the raiding attempts of the Distillery Workers. We referred to the union officers who had quit their union post without any notice or explanation, and then urged workers to leave our union. We did not denounce them, rather saying they had been misled by all kinds of irresponsible promises. We expressed regret that those who had held top union positions for more than three years had seen fit to attempt to destroy what they had helped build. We also said that, as we were the sole bargaining agent, we would continue looking after the workers' daily problems in accordance with the contract as we had always done. We announced the names of the temporary officers and Dalpe's appointment as business agent. We concluded with Percy Bengough's remark about booze and rubber not mixing.

Instead of handing circulars out at the plant gate, we posted them on the bulletin boards in all departments. This was our right under the union contract, and it was not available to Fournier, who had to remain outside the plant gate. It was evidence that we were "in" and he was "out." The announcement was widely discussed and President Bengough's "mixer" statement created a greater reaction than we expected. Many not only regarded it as humourous, but also questioned the logic of joining a distillery union.

The next step was to demonstrate that we were continuing our normal bargaining relationship with the company. I arranged to meet with the plant manager, Clarence Headcraft, to introduce our new officers and business agent. I also wanted to discuss a suitable timetable for our forthcoming negotiations for a new agreement.

"Aren't you having some trouble with Mr. Fournier?" Headcraft asked.

"No." I replied. "He may be in some difficulty with us. We are the recognized bargaining union in your plant, and we remain so until another union officially and legally replaces us. So, until such time, we will continue to exercise our normal responsibilities."

We then agreed on a date for the meeting. When we entered Headcraft's office he had greeted us with his usual nervous, twitching smile. He was a short, energetic man, who always seemed under great stress. He generally spoke in loud, animated, and clipped phrases. Our discussions were, as usual, conducted in English, although with one or two exceptions none of the union officers spoke or understood English. In deference to them the bilingual personnel officer, Forbes Kennedy, gave a rough translation of the remarks.

Throughout this period of inter-union rivalry the company lived up to its legal obligation to our union. On the day of our meeting with Headcraft there was more than the usual discussion and excitement in the plant. The meeting certainly strengthened our position.

But shortly after there was an unexpected and shocking development. Fournier managed to obtain a court order in the form of an interlocutory injunction preventing our union from having any contractual dealings with the company or receiving union dues, which were collected by checkoff. When Paul Dalpe telephoned to tell me the injunction had been served, I was stunned. I could hardly believe that a union representative would obtain an injunction against another union, a tactic employed by anti-union companies against unions. It was a practice that was generally condemned by the labour movement, with strong demands that court injunctions not be allowed in industrial disputes.

In many years in the labour movement, no single event affected me more deeply than that injunction. I was outraged, scandalized, and ashamed that one of my colleagues would stoop to such a level. After I spoke with Dalpe I remember sitting brooding in my office, and saying to myself: "How could he, how could he, that son-of-a-bitch."

With our lawyer, Guy Merrill Desaulnier, I rushed off to St. Jérôme and met with our union officers. Desaulnier read the conditions of the injunction and explained that the court had put a temporary restraint on our bargaining rights because Fournier had claimed that the Distillery Workers, and not our TLC local, represented a majority of the employees. The injunction specified that a court hearing would be held shortly to ascertain which of the two unions actually represented a majority.

With this development I saw a good opportunity for calling a membership meeting. In a few hours we prepared a circular and distributed it at the plant gate, informing the workers that, because of the injunction which Fournier had obtained, our union was temporarily prevented from representing them when they had grievances or complaints. Also, negotiations for a new contract were for the time being suspended. We announced a membership meeting at which the situation would be fully explained. The meeting would also discuss demands which we would present to the company in the forthcoming negotiations.

Normally, a meeting at which a new contract is to be discussed is well attended, and we hoped that would be the case. We were not disappointed; the auditorium above the fire hall was solidly packed. Desaulnier, in his customary meticulous manner, explained the meaning and condition of the injunction. Understandingly, he made no personal observations regarding the merits of the injunctions and his explanation was confined solely to the legal aspects.

Paul Dalpe, on the other hand, made a fiery and articulate speech. He pointed out that, as of the day the injunction was served, and so long as it remained in effect, no union officer, no shop steward could represent the workers. Anyone who had a grievance could have to handle it himself. "And who is responsible for that?" he shouted. All negotiations for a new contract were suspended. "And who is responsible for that?" he asked again. "And who gains by all this? The company. And who loses by all this? You and you and you and all the workers in Dominion."

It was the best, and certainly the most effective speech I ever heard him make. He succeeded in reaching the workers' minds and at the same time touched their hearts. Cheers and applause punctuated his speech, becoming increasingly loud and more frequent. I believed we had reached a significant turning point in our campaign to retain the local. As I observed the reaction of the members, it became apparent that the more than 500 people present were outraged by the injunction affair.

Strangely, discussion on the new contract began with little enthusiasm. It was obvious that the workers were not in a very receptive mood to consider contractual questions. We suggested that departmental meetings be convened later to go over suggestions for the new contract. When the meeting adjourned, small groups gathered to talk about the situation. I was convinced that we had a solid core of support.

While we waited for the court hearing, we held small meetings of representatives of the different departments. Even there the main topic of interest was the injunction and the difficulties it had created. In the meantime Fournier applied to the Department of Labour for the certification of his union. The court hearing was finally held in September with Judge Cousineau presiding. Desaulnier was our lawyer and Fournier was represented by André Montpetit. Some years later, both lawyers became distinguished judges, and Montpetit represented the University of Montreal on the Board of Governors of the Labour College of Canada and was chairman of the Executive Committee.

At one of the sittings there was an unfortunate incident which has remained with me all my life. During a recess I walked over to where Montpetit was sitting. I knew him well as he had acted as chairman of arbitration boards, and I regarded him as a very honourable and ethical person. Now he was involved in a deal that was not kosher, and he knew it. I said: "André, you don't give a damn who you defend, do you?"

He did not reply, but slowly he turned to face me. In his narrowed 'yes' and the slight twitch of his mouth, I saw the deep wound my remarks had made. He got up from his chair, turned his back on me, and walked away without a word. I realized at once that my remark was stupid and unforgivable. I don't know what possessed me to make it, other than a pent-up feeling that moved me to hit out at something or someone. Why I was questioning his integrity I do not know. I felt ashamed, and ready to run away and hide. When I regained my senses I approached him again, and holding out my hand apologized for my remark. He seemed to sense my shame and regret, and being a kind man he smiled, shook my hand, and simply said: "Max, don't take life so seriously."

After several sessions the hearings ended and Judge Cousineau took the case under consideration. To the best of my knowledge a decision has yet to be rendered, some 40 years later.

In October 1946 we were advised that the Department of Labour would conduct a vote among the employees to determine which of the two unions they wanted to represent them. The days leading up to this vote were tense. We formed a number of small groups to visit their fellow workers in their homes, urging them to vote for our union. We were also fortunate in having a number of energetic women who campaigned for us tirelessly.

I never took a vote for granted, and although our officers were fairly confident of the result, I was less certain. I felt that the vote would be close, at best, and it still could go either way. I kept encouraging our people not to slacken their efforts. Dalpe was at the plant gate morning, noon, and evening, beaming confidence. On the day of the vote I was in my room in the Lapointe Hotel, nervous, impatient, and feeling the first symptoms of a stomach ulcer.

Finally, when the ballots were counted, the result was decisive: we won with a substantial majority. Our supporters came running out of the plant laughing, shouting, and congratulating each other. Dalpe and I were there greeting and thanking them for their support. Those who we knew had not supported us we befriended. Everyone was happy that the division in the plant, the squabbles and arguments, had finally ended. That night we celebrated at the Lapointe Hotel, and no union celebration in St. Jérôme since has exceeded the merriment of that night.

The following day, when I became physically and emotionally able, I telephoned President Bengough to tell him the result. He was naturally pleased.

The vote automatically terminated the restraints on our bargaining rights. We resumed negotiations and eventually signed a new agreement. Soon the union settled down to normal activities. Paul Dalpe remained in his post for several years, and then resigned for personal reasons. He was replaced by Marcel Charbonneau, who was a member of our Executive Committee. Charbonneau was not as effervescent as Dalpe, but he was a very intelligent, serious man. His sincerity and deep belief in the labour movement and in human rights was recognized by all who knew him. He died at his post as a TLC organizer for St. Jérôme when he was only 40 years of age. He was a competent, humble, good man and he was greatly missed.

The union remained active as a chartered local of the TLC until the 1956 merger of the Trades and Labour Congress and the Canadian Congress of Labour. It then became part of the United Rubber Workers' International Union, an affiliate of the CLC.

I want to add a footnote to that memorable event in St. Jérôme in 1946. From all I have written about Paul Fournier the reader may conclude that he was some kind of a sinister and miserable character. A character he was, but sinister or miserable he was not. In fact he was a charming, colourful, and even flamboyant kind of a person. He may not have known the heroic virtues of life, but he loved life intensely and he had great capacity for living boldly and sometimes defiantly. He was reasonably competent in his work as a union official and was always ready to help colleagues. Yet he was impatient and sometimes impetuous: the machine-gun delivery of his words sometimes preceded his thoughts. He remained a colleague and friend until the day he died in his early 50s.

MURDOCHVILLE

MURDOCHVILLE IS A COMMUNITY that was carved out of the wilderness in the heart of the Gaspé Peninsula. The Gaspé Copper Mine, a subsidiary of Noranda Mines, is located just outside the town.

Shortly after the company began operating, in the early 1950s, the United Steelworkers of America (CCL-CIO) began organizing the workers. A majority signed up and the union applied to the Quebec Labour Board for certification. The company opposed the application on the ground that it was not yet in full production. The Board supported the company's position and rejected the application.

Several months later one of the employees came to my office in Montreal. He told me he wanted to see the workers organized and he would be glad to assist us in establishing a union. He wanted to know if the TLC would be interested. He told me about the Steelworkers' efforts, and said that after the rejection of their application the organizers had left, and had not been heard of since. After a long discussion I told him I would discuss the matter with the Congress and would be in touch with him shortly.

I had mixed feelings about becoming involved. There were several problems: first, I personally could not undertake such a campaign, as I was shortly to be transferred to the TLC headquarters in Ottawa, and the three other organizers in Quebec were fully involved in other organizing activities. Secondly, the anti-union reputation of Noranda Mines was well-known, and I was sure the company would make every effort to block us. Finally, what if the Steelworkers were to return to Murdochville in the course of the campaign? In those days the TLC did not provide funds for organizing activities. Beyond such expenses as travelling for organizers, there was quite simply no additional money available.

I knew all too well that we could not possibly cope with a determined opposition by the company and a concentrated drive by the Steelworkers. I pondered these problems for several days. The fact was that I was not so much concerned about being opposed by the company, or the political influence which I knew the company could exercize. Rather, I was very much concerned about the possibility of getting into a battle with the Steelworkers. Yet I had no way of knowing whether they would return.

Finally, I decided to recommend to President Bengough that we undertake a campaign at Gaspé Copper. What intrigued me most about the challenge was the imminent development of a frontier community. I had a romantic notion about the birth of a new town, visualizing powerful machines cutting roads and streets out of the wilderness, laying water mains and sewage drains, erecting buildings and houses, putting up power lines. With all this I could see a stream of people coming with new hopes and dreams for a better life. Of course I wanted to organize the miners, but I also wanted to know and feel the excitement of the birth of a new community.

When I met President Bengough, I naturally did not express these sentiments. I gave him a detailed account of the situation, the experience of the Steelworkers, and the request I had from the Gaspé miners. I recommended that we undertake the drive, assigning Bernard Boulanger, who was stationed in Quebec City, as organizer. As usual Bengough listened very attentively to my full explanation, but when he began to blink and reached for another cigarette I knew he was becoming a bit impatient, and that I had not convinced him. He asked me exactly where Murdochville was, and when I told him he asked if it was not too far.

"Too far from where?" I asked. "Chief, ten years ago when you designated the Province of Quebec as my territory I'm sure you meant the whole province, not only part of it. Murdochville and the Gaspé Copper Mine are in Quebec, and I respectfully recommend that we try to organize these workers."

Then my romantic sentiments about the new town emerged. I talked about the possibility of hundreds, perhaps thousands, of construction workers being involved in the development. I suggested we could invite the building trade unions to go to Murdochville and we could help them organize. I was speaking rapidly, carried away by my enthusiasm. When I finally stopped, there was silence. The President got out of his chair and paced his office several times. Then he sat down in a chair next to me, and spoke slowly:

"Max, I don't want to take the wind out of your sails, but let me ask you, if Noranda defeated the United Steelworkers of America, what makes you think they will not defeat you?"

"We will never know if we don't try," I said.

"What if you get into a clash with the company?"

"If I'm not able to handle it I'll come to you for help."

"When you do I'll not be of much help," he warned. "You know that we just don't have the means to support strikes or pay legal fees or arbitration board expenses."

"Of course, I do," I said, "but I don't see a strike situation yet. In fact I have no idea if we can succeed in signing up a majority of the workers, but if we do, and if the company pulls political strings to prevent us from becoming certified, then we too can pull some strings."

"What do you mean?"

"Well, I believe in that kind of a setting the only one in the government to talk to would be Premier Duplessis."

"What makes you think you can see Premier Duplessis?"

"I can't, but you can," I replied.

I knew he did not expect that observation. He blinked again, furrowed his brow, and seemed about to say something, but I went on:

"Chief, I don't mean that some deal should be made with Duplessis. I mean that if we actually succeed in organizing a majority of the workers and apply for certification in full compliance with the law, then we can ask the Premier to use his good offices to assure that our application will not be denied."

"Max, I am dubious about seeing Duplessis on such an issue," he said after a long pause.

"Of course we are assuming that Duplessis would have to be seen," I said. "On the other hand it may not come to that. If he does have to be seen, then I respectfully suggest that you would not see him on the issue of our application for certification. I believe you could quite legitimately be in Quebec City on Congress business and arrange a courtesy call on the Premier. I think, from what I know of him, and with the help of the Minister of Labour, Duplessis would be very happy to receive you. In the course of the conversation you could, *en passant*, mention the Murdochville affair, and then see what happens.

The President smiled, and then pointing a long finger at me said: "You really want to organize that mine, don't you Max?"

"Yes, Chief."

"Go ahead," he said.

I asked Bernard Boulanger to go to Murdochville to see what contacts he could make and to determine the general situation with regard to organizing. He returned about a week later and said that, although he had not been allowed to go near the mine site, he had seen a number of workers in their homes. He said some were eager to join the union, but others were apprehensive about the chances of a union being established. With some caution he said he thought we should initiate a campaign. I suggested he arrange his affairs in Quebec City and then return to Murdochville as soon as it was convenient. About two weeks after he arrived back in Murdochville he telephoned to tell me he had signed up about 100 members and was ready to apply to the Congress for a local union charter. I thought he had done exceedingly well in such a short time and I congratulated him.

When Boulanger's application for a charter was received at Congress head-quarters it caused some eyebrow-raising. He had named the union "The International Union of Mine Workers in Gaspé." Never had a TLC federally-chartered union been called "international." Nevertheless, because of the peculiar situation in Quebec, the charter was so inscribed, and Federal Local number 245 was born.

Slowly but steadily more and more workers joined. When the first membership meeting was called I went and also asked Fred Doucet, a TLC organizer at Fredericton, N.B., to attend. Since there were no hotels or motels, we stayed at a fishing camp at York Lake, some six miles from the mine site.

The meeting was held in an old shack that belonged to one of the building contractors, and it was better attended than we anticipated. The following day I returned to Ottawa, where I was then located as the director of organization and education.

Doucet remained for a few days, assisting Boulanger. Three months later, when a majority had joined, we applied for certification. Several weeks went by, and then we were stunned when we were advised that the Board had rejected our application.

I spoke to the labour representative on the Board, Marcel Franq. He assured me there were no irregularities, but said we were two cards short of an overall majority.

It would have been simple to sign up two more members, but it didn't work that way. Once our application was rejected we would have to make a new application, and this meant signing all new cards for submission to the Board. Having come so close we decided to renew our campaign and began signing the members on new cards. We told them of the Board's decision and our determination to continue our efforts to win bargaining rights. In the meantime some of the workers had left and others had come. Getting them to sign new cards was not easy. They had signed Steelworkers' cards, then they signed TLC cards, and now we were asking them to sign yet another card. Some were disenchanted with unions, others were discouraged, and still others felt that as long as the company and the government were determined to keep a union out of the Gaspé they would succeed, for the present at least. The workers' morale was low, but we continued with our campaign. Victor Trudeau, our organizer in Montreal, assisted Boulanger as much as possible.

The campaign progressed slowly, and I thought the time had come to exercize some political pressure. I discussed the matter with President Bengough. He said he would be willing to arrange a meeting with Premier Duplessis, but only after we actually obtained a majority and filed a new application for certification. I agreed.

We increased the momentum of the drive, holding more meetings, and distributing more circulars. Trudeau and Boulanger spent more time in the area. It took about four months to sign up what we knew was a substantial majority, and it was in February 1954 that we made a second application for certification. In the meantime arrangements were made for President Bengough to pay a courtesy call on Premier Duplessis in Quebec City, and I accompanied him. This was the first time they had met, and the Premier was cordial, talkative, and characteristically jovial. He had a quick mind and an extraordinary sense of humour, particularly on political issues and personalities.

I cannot recall that any serious issues or situations were discussed. Neither the Premier nor the President raised any subject that tended to be controversial, although there were many such in Quebec at the time. It was mainly small talk.

After about half an hour President Bengough felt it was time to leave, and he got around to the new copper mine at Murdochville, casually mentioning that the Congress staff had been trying to organize the workers there for the past six months, and that an application for certification had been filed with the Labour Board. He then turned to me, as though he was not quite sure, and asked:

"Max, we did file an application, did we not?"

"Yes," I said, and then looking at the Premier, continued, "In fact this is our second application, Mr. Premier. When we first applied some four months ago we did not, apparently, quite have an overall majority. We renewed our efforts and this time we are absolutely sure we have a substantial majority of the workers signed up."

Addressing the Premier, President Bengough commented: "I don't anticipate any problem for our union to be certified." It was more of a question than a statement of fact. The Premier asked whether we had heard from the Board, and when we said we had not, he offered to try to determine from Judge Horace Boivin, the chairman, whether the application had been considered. In a few minutes he had Judge Boivin on the telephone and, speaking English, I am sure out of courtesy to us, said:

"Mr. Bengough, you know, the President of the Trades and Labour Congress of Canada, and his representative in Quebec (he either forgot or could not pronounce my name) are in my office. They are interested in knowing whether you have already considered their application for certification for the copper mine in the Gaspé."

He listened for a few minutes and then asked: "The application will be considered this week?" I was not sure whether it was a question or a command. He thanked the judge for the information and hung up. Looking at us with his sharp but smiling eyes, he remarked: "I am very pleased to have such an honourable and kind gentleman as Judge Boivin as chairman of our Labour Board."

President Bengough thanked the Premier for the information. The Premier thanked the President for dropping in. We shook hands and left. On 26 May 1954, we were advised that the International Union of Mine Workers in Gaspé has been certified as the exclusive bargaining agency. There was never any doubt in my mind that a good majority of the workers had joined the union, but I was equally convinced that our courtesy call on Premier Duplessis helped considerably in getting the certification.

Shortly after we received the official certification, we arranged to begin negotiating the first collective agreement for the Gaspé miners. The local union officers, with Boulanger and myself, met with the local plant manger, a Mr. Bressendon. Our first meeting was not a very happy experience. Although we did not expect the company to receive us with open arms, we did expect common courtesy and a reasonable effort to negotiate an agreement in good faith.

We soon found our expectations on both counts were unfounded. Bressendon did not, or could not, agree to the most inconsequential clauses in our proposed contract. As we slowly read our proposals, clause by clause, there were long periods of silence as we waited for the company's reaction. In fact there was no reaction. He would finally say: "We will have to think about that."

In fact, Bressendon seemed bored and disinterested in the whole exercise. When I finally finished reading the contract, he repeated that he would have to discuss it further and give it a great deal of thought. He would let us know in due course. When I wanted to arrange a date for another bargaining session he said he could not agree on a date at that time. He would let the local union president know when it would be convenient for the company to meet with us.

It had become obvious very early in the so-called bargaining session that Bressendon lacked any authority whatsoever. I had the feeling that he had been instructed from Toronto neither to agree nor to bargain. I suspected that even his cool and indifferent behaviour was a prearranged scenario.

I then decided to by-pass Bressendon and meet with the company general manager in Toronto, a Mr. Porrit. That meeting began in an unusual and disturbing manner. When I entered his office he was at his desk writing. I naturally expected that he would at least acknowledge my presence, and perhaps even shake hands. He did neither. As I stood in front of his desk he spoke in a mumble without even lifting his eyes: "I'll be with you in a minute, Mr. Swerdlow."

He continued writing and did not even ask me to sit down. I just stood in front of his desk, feeling very silly, and, in fact, insulted. My mind flashed back to the company's similar behaviour in the Gaspé about two week earlier, and I concluded the company was playing the same kind of psychological game in both Gaspé and Toronto. I was angry, damn angry, but I contained my emotions. Above all, I wanted a collective agreement, and so I swallowed my pride, at least up to a point.

After a few minutes Porrit put aside his writing and looked up at me. I didn't wait for him to ask me to sit down, I just pulled a chair over to his desk and sat down. I do not have any record of that meeting, but I recall that conversation vividly. I spoke politely, but directly, and with firmness. I told him that it was my opinion that any further meetings or negotiations with Bressendon at Gaspé would be a waste of time — both his and mine. I continued: "I know that in such matters as union contracts he does only what you instruct him to do, and so why don't we negotiate now, at least on the main issues? If we reach an agreement then we can go through the motions of negotiation when I return to Gaspé. Mr. Porrit, as you are the general manager of Gaspé, you must be a practical man. I, as director of organization and education for the Trades and Labour Congress of Canada, regard myself to be a practical person. Then why don't we cut out the playing around, and let us try to agree on a contract that we can both live with?"

He did not reply immediately. He just stared at me with a rather puzzled look. I don't think he expected either my attitude or my proposition. Then, much to my surprise, his deadpan expression gave way to a faint, but not unpleasant smile, and he spoke. "All right Mr. Swerdlow, let's negotiate."

We made a short list of union demands, and then began to discuss them, with the understanding that anything I agreed to would be subject to approval by the union in Gaspé. He had no quarrel with that condition.

We compromised on a number of clauses, such as seniority and a grievance procedure. On our demand for a wage increase and more paid holidays he was not ready to give a definite figure, but he felt we could reach agreement on both matters. However, on our demand for the Rand Formula, which would provide a check-off of union dues by all employees, union and non-union, covered by the agreement, he was adamantly opposed. I presented all the well-known arguments in support of the formula, and he, in turn, presented the usual management arguments in opposition. His main point was that the Gaspé operation was in the process of building its permanent labour force, and therefore, for some time there would continue to be a steady turnover of employees. Consequently, the company felt it could not be tied down by the Rand Formula.

"If we dropped our demand for the Rand Formula, would you agree to a check-off of union dues?" I asked.

"No," he replied emphatically.

"In that case, we have no choice but to submit our entire contract to arbitration,"

I said.

"If that is your choice, go ahead."

"What about wages?"

He stared at me for a moment before he replied.

"Mr. Swerdlow, drop your demand for the Rand Formula and the check-off of union dues and I believe you will accept our offer on the matter of wages."

I told him there was no chance in hell that we would drop our demand for, at the least, the check-off. Nevertheless, I would discuss this with the President of the Congress and with the Gaspé workers, but first I would have to have a figure on wages and holidays. He said he would get in touch with me in a few days, and that was the end of our meeting.

Several days later he telephoned me and said that Bressendon had been authorized to state the company's position on wages and holidays, as well as other contractual issues, but, under no circumstance would they concede in any way, shape, or form to the Rand Formula or a check-off.

I asked whether the offer Bressendon would make was the company's final offer, or whether there was room for negotiation. He answered: "Mr. Swerdlow, I believe that you are a practical man, as you said, and will accept our offer. Consequently, I see no reason for making several offers and wasting a lot of time bargaining. I just want you to bear in mind that everything is negotiable, except — and I repeat — the matter of the check-off of union dues."

I telephoned Boulanger and told him to arrange a meeting with Bressendon. When we met he was only slightly more cordial than he had been at the first session. He made a few concessions on some contractual clauses, but rejected other clauses without making any recommendation. He offered a general wage increase of 15 cents an hour and five paid holidays. When he finished outlining the company's offer he quietly added: "Gentlemen, the company's offer is a package deal on a two-year agreement. As far as we are concerned there is no need for further discussion. If you accept the package, we can sign a collective agreement; if you don't, then you can do what you think best."

He folded his papers, as if to indicate that the session had ended. What arrogance, I thought. I tried to negotiate. I asked for what reason the company rejected several clauses which I pointed to. He replied that the company had "good reasons." Try as I would, I could not move him. Finally, as I was both frustrated and impatient, I said: "You make an offer, and then you say, 'Take it or leave it.' Surely this is not negotiating in good faith." He replied: "I wouldn't say, Mr. Swerdlow, that we are not negotiating in good faith. Certainly we are. On the other hand, you are quite right in your remark about taking it or leaving it."

I knew of course, that he had no authority but to follow the instructions he had received from the head office, and that any further discussion would be futile. I said I would submit the offer to our members and would be in touch with the company as soon as the membership reached a decision.

We hurriedly convened a meeting that same evening. For the first time in more than ten years of negotiating I was recommending acceptance of a company's final offer, and I was not very happy about it. I was quite satisfied with the wage offer and the holidays, but not with most of the other clauses, and particularly the absence of any form of union security. Considering the sprawling nature of the mining operation, I knew that the collection of union dues would be very difficult, and I realized that if the dues were not collected the union would be hard pressed to carry on its work.

But what options did we have? If we had the means we would have gone to arbitration, and I think we would have a more favourable decision on a number of the issues, but we did not have the means. On the matter of wages, I doubted whether we could have got more. Furthermore, had we received a very good decision, and should the company reject it, as I suspected they would, we were not in a position to strike.

I consoled myself by reasoning that, after all, this was our first contract, and we had succeeded in establishing bargaining rights in the Gaspé when, before us the powerful Steelworkers' Union had failed. I thought legal bargaining rights were paramount, and that eventually, we would improve the agreement. When I concluded my report and recommendation to the members, they voted to accept the company's package. The first collective agreement in the Gaspé was signed a few days after the meeting.

In the months that followed the local union officers were more or less left to carry on with union activities as best they could. From time to time they called on our organizers when they felt they needed assistance, but generally the local was not a very viable operation. In the meantime the merger of the two Congresses to form the Canadian Labour Congress was pending. Before our two-year agreement was up for renewal we made arrangement with Pat Burke and Bob Levesque, the Quebec Director and Organizer of the Steelworkers, to transfer the Gaspé local to their union.

What followed, including a long and bitter strike, has been amply recorded. Some who have written about these events have failed to mention that the Trades and Labour Congress was, in fact, the first to establish a union in the Gaspé. It has also been written: "A year later the International Union of Mine Employees, newly chartered by the TLC, arrived on the scene, *apparently with the support of the company and government*, since it rapidly obtained certification and a two-year agreement."

Obviously, the author of that quotation did not know the facts, nor did he take the trouble to ascertain them. The result was his unkind and completely false accusation. I never pretended to be proud of the agreement I signed in Gaspé Copper. Nevertheless, our union finally was established, became recognized, and collective bargaining began.

CHAPTER SIX
The Merger

I REMAINED THE TRADES AND LABOUR CONGRESS district representative in Quebec for ten years, and during that time I was engaged in a multitude of duties: organizing, negotiating, presenting cases to conciliation and arbitration boards, settling grievances, being involved in strikes, and generally being active in all phases of the labour movement. My life was full of exciting and rewarding experiences.

From the early 1940s through the 1950s trade union membership in Canada increased dramatically. It went from 362,000 in 1940 to 832,000 in 1946, and passed the million mark, reaching 1,029,000 in 1951, then up to 1,459,000 in 1959. The TLC organizing staff in Quebec was enlarged and organizers were added in other provinces. In order to give more direction to the bigger staff, and to co-ordinate their activities, a new position was created — National Director of Organization. I was offered the post, which meant moving to Ottawa.

Needless to say, I was thrilled. Before I actually moved, an article appeared in the *Montreal Gazette* announcing my appointment. It said I was to be "Director of Organization and Education," though there had been no discussion about my involvement in education. I telephoned Percy Bengough to inquire because the announcement had come from his office.

"Chief," I said, "What is the meaning of this announcement? Am I to be responsible for education as well as organization?"

"Well," he replied, "Don't worry about it. When you have nothing to do in organization you can do some educational work."

And that was how I became the TLC Director of both Organization and Education in 1952.

Percy Bengough was nearing the end of his term as president, a position to which he had first been elected in 1942. The official announcement of his resignation was to be made at the 1954 convention, and I thought our national staff should demonstrate their appreciation of his remarkable service. But what was appropriate, surely not another silver tray or a pair of gold cuff-links? Then I had an idea. He had always written his own editorial for the Congress monthly *Journal*, and I thought a bound copy of the editorials, spanning a period of twelve years, might be both appropriate and unusual. I discussed the idea with some colleagues, as well as with Secretary-Treasurer Gordon Cushing, and they all approved. Shortly before the convention the volume was completed, and with the assistance of another colleague, Leslie Wismer, I wrote a foreword and then we had the volume bound and encased.

Shortly before the convention adjourned I went to the platform, accompanied by 20 staff members. As I read the forward, there was a silence. I had a lump in my throat and had to stop for what seemed like a long time to contain my emotion.

This, in part, was the foreword:

Dear Brother President,

It is not unusual for the first edition of an author's work to begin with a foreword by some admiring advocate.... Such promotional activity has a two-fold purpose of introducing a new author to the literary world, and at the same time attempting to assure his future employment and adequate income.... The author here needs no such introduction. Nor is there any problem about his future employment....

Those who have read these editorials have been impressed, not only with the simple language; but also with the careful detail, extensive research, and clear thinking they manifest.... Indeed, these editorials are not a subject for debate; but a road to follow....

These articles span a dozen years, in which you have so successfully led the Trades and Labour Congress of Canada, and followed its development and growth from a robust adolescent into the fully mature and reliable manhood which we are so proud to be a part of....

We have never thought of you as our employer or general manager, although we greatly admire and have benefitted from your excellent executive abilities. You are our brother, and as brothers we have worked with you for the common cause of organized men and women....

In these 12 years the waters have not always been calm. When you assumed leadership of the Congress in 1942, our country was in the midst of a terrible war. As President of the Trades and Labour Congress of Canada you encouraged and inspired the workers of Canada to greater war efforts.... Your leadership in this regard won for you the admiration of all people and the recognition of the Crown. We are proud indeed that you possess the star and ribbon emblematic of such companionship. We are also proud that you have been recognized and honoured by two distinguished universities for your contribution to the improvement of our Canadian way of life....

We sincerely hope that the pen which shaped ... the following pages will continue to be active so that our goal may be the sooner reached, when all who toil will be secure and when, in the exercise of our rights and freedoms, the dignity of man becomes unquestioned. We know we speak for all when we say: "Brother President, thank you for a job wonderfully done."

This was signed by the entire staff.

The labour movement in Canada had reached one of the most significant turning points in its history. When the 1955 convention was held, plans were well advanced for a merger between the Trades and Labour Congress of Canada and the Canadian Congress of Labour to bring into being one central body, the Canadian Labour Congress. All hopes were that this would end the years of struggle and strife between the two organizations, dating back to 1939. That was the convention which had caused me such distress in silently witnessing the expulsion of seven unions, which later became the nucleus of the Canadian Congress of Labour (CCL), and in the United States, the Congress of Industrial Organizations (CIO).

Now, in 1955 at Windsor, that situation was to be corrected. In the intervening 16 years relations between the TLC and the CCL had been cool. Some unions in both congresses had stretched their jurisdictions to attract workers away from unions in the opposing congress. Internecine raiding was all too frequent.

Despite this unfortunate state of affairs there were leaders in both congresses who favoured a more positive attitude, with the eventual objective of bringing about a merger. The 1944 TLC convention had instructed the officers seriously to study the possibility of establishing one central body, with the qualification that any such move should provide "proper safeguards for all unions with regard to their jurisdictional rights."

Progress was slow. In 1950 a Joint National Consultative Committee and Co-operative Council was formed, with representation from both congresses, to facilitate co-operation in areas of mutual interest. The effort met with little success. Then, in 1953, a Unity Committee was formed, composed of the four top officers of each congress, to explore the possibilities of organic union. In the same year there was agreement on a "No Raiding Pact," to curb jurisdictional disputes and raiding practices.

These actions paralleled discussions in the Untied States between the AFL and the CIO. In both countries there was growing concern within the respective labour movements at the failure to increase union membership. A good deal of effort was directed to raiding, resulting in a form of musical chairs, with the membership shuffled from one union to another, while the total overall union membership remained static, or showed only minor gain.

In Canada, despite a mutual interest in many matters of common concern, there was a marked difference between the two congresses. These were, to some extent, reflected in the personalities of the individuals who headed the two organizations. Percy Bengough had the stature of a statesman. He had easy access to Prime Minister Mackenzie King and his Cabinet. Bengough believed in the diplomatic approach and was opposed to direct partisan political action on the part of organized labour. On the other hand, the Canadian Congress of Labour was headed by Aaron R. Mosher, founder of the Canadian Brotherhood of Railway Employees (CBRE). He was a more flamboyant character, an ardent and vocal critic of the government, and a strong advocate of direct political action by unions. He was an avowed socialist and one of the founders of the Co-operative Commonwealth Federation (CCF), the predecessor of the New Democratic Party (NDP).

In the merger the TLC was indisputably the senior partner. It was the older (1883 vs. 1940), and the larger (600,000 vs. 400,000). While overlapping union jurisdictions remained a major hurdle, there was also the matter of established personalities and their positions. In Canada this was resolved at the top by the retirement of both Bengough and Mosher. In the United States there was a more macabre solution: both William Green, president of the AFL, and Philip Murray, president of the CIO, died within a short space of time.

The fact that there was a strong movement toward a merger of the two congresses in the United States had an important bearing in Canada. Without it powerful international unions might have used their influence to prevent such a development in Canada, just as they had used it in 1939 to bring about the expulsion of seven unions from the TLC.

Now, at the TLC's 1955 convention, Secretary-Treasurer Gordon Cushing stood on a platform at the Windsor Armoury reading the Unity Committee's report recommending a merger. He was a somewhat pedantic and monotonous speaker, but as he read the document there were traces of emotion in his voice. Like most of the delegates he was deeply moved by the significance of what he was involved in.

The delegates sat motionless and silent as they listened. My own thoughts went back to 1939. There, on the platform at Windsor, was Carl Berg, the man who with such a sad heart had placed before the 1939 convention the motion to expel the CIO unions. How vividly I remembered my feeling of guilt for not having spoken out against the resolution. Now, 16 years later, the labour movement was about to be reunited, and I felt I had to speak in support of the unity report. I was no longer the shy and impressionable young novice of 1939. Now I was the TLC Director of Organization and Education and a seasoned labour official.

When Cushing finished reading the report, the first delegate recognized, to open the debate, was Frank Hall, vice-president of the Brotherhood of Railway and Steamship Clerks, Freight Handlers, Express, and Station Employees. This was appropriate. Frank Hall and his union had been deeply involved in jurisdictional battles, most particularly with Mosher's CBRE, and he had been responsible for the expulsion of that union from the TLC. Now he was sounding the keynote for the convention's endorsement of the Unity Report, which means a healing of old wounds.

Frank Hall was a highly effective speaker; forcefully and eloquently he challenged, reasoned, and pleaded for full and unequivocal endorsement, saying in part:

We stand here at a time when every man must stand up and be counted, and I, for one, am prepared to stand up and be counted, and say that I am whole-heartedly in favour of this proposal to merge these two national bodies. The time has come to re-establish once again solidarity in the ranks of the workers in this country, so that we may have unity and we may have co-operation and we may carry on with a united voice and with a guarantee of an even greater degree of success for our movement. I appeal to this convention to unanimously support the recommendation.

When he finished speaking there was loud and prolonged applause. The second speaker was Douglas Hamilton, a member of the United Brotherhood of Carpenters and Joiners and a vice-president of the Toronto and District Trades and Labour Council. He also spoke in favour of the report.

Then I was recognized. My contribution to the discussion was not intended to be a plea for support of the report for it was already evident that it would be overwhelmingly endorsed. However, I could not resist referring to the 1939 expulsion and the sad legacy it had left behind for so many years. I went on:

Mr. Chairman, I remember the first convention of this Congress that I attended 16 years ago. At that time the convention made a very profound impression on me. I was naturally 16 years younger and it was the first time I had attended a labour gathering with so many people in attendance. I vividly remember the chairman of the Resolutions Committee bringing in a resolution suspending a group of people, a group or organizations, from the Trades and Labour Congress.

The man who had that unpleasant task sits on your platform today. It was Carl Berg who was the chairman on the Resolution Committee. After he brought that resolution in, Carl Berg practically broke down and cried. There was no joy in his voice and no happiness in his heart when he moved concurrence in that resolution. I have been associated with Carl Berg over these 16 years, and every time that convention is brought up for discussion, Carl Berg always said: "I hope I will be attending a convention when I will see the Congress recommend unification of the two labour bodies in Canada." Carl, your wish is coming true, for today I hope this convention will vote in favour of unity.

The remainder of my speech, as well as those of others, is in the official Report of Proceedings.

A number of delegates spoke, most in support of the report, with only a few expressing reservations. Then the vote was taken. Technically the report was adopted unanimously, since no one voted against it. Actually a small group of "old timers" abstained from voting. When the chairman declared the report adopted unanimously, pandemonium broke out in the convention hall.

Frank Hall's participation in the historic event had not ended. There was a significant development the following day, which few witnessed. Following adoption of the United Report, the convention had immediately extended an invitation to A.R. Mosher in Ottawa to come to Windsor and address the convention as a fraternal delegate. As he stepped off the train at the Windsor station, Frank Hall was waiting on the platform to greet and shake the hand of his long-time opponent.

The same day the Windsor newspaper *The Border City Star* had a cartoon depicting some TLC officials in the process of building a new united labour centre. I was pictured, huddled between Percy Bengough and Claude Jodoin, with Gordon Cushing standing rather detached a short distance away. I suspected that the artist knew how cool Cushing really was to the merger.

While the retirement of Bengough and Mosher had facilitated the change of command, there was still the matter of selecting a president for the new congress. There was no division of opinion. Claude Jodoin, a member of the International Ladies' Garment Workers' Union (ILGWU) and a prominent Quebec trade unionist, had succeeded Bengough as President of the TLC, and there was unanimous agreement that he, as president of the larger and older congress, should be the first president of the new CLC.

He was one of the enthusiastic architects of the new body, but at the same time, he respected the feeling of those who did not share his enthusiasm. He fully appreciated the historic significance of presiding over the last convention of the TLC and he had not taken it lightly by any means.

Claude Jodoin was a big man, well over six feet tall, with close to 300 well-distributed pounds. With his dark, neatly-groomed hair and large, soft, but expressive eyes, he looked strong, authoritative, and impressive. He moved slowly, with deliberation, swaying gently from side to side. He was an obvious extrovert; a gregarious, animated, and generous man. He seemed to love all mankind. His ready and contagious laughter exploded with the force and sound of rolling thunder, and when sentiment moved him his large eyes easily teared.

From the time he joined the organizing staff of the ILGWU in Montreal in 1936, he rose rapidly in the labour movement, holding various positions of increasing importance and responsibility. He became president of the Montreal Trades and

Labour Council (1947-1954), president of the TLC (1954-1956), and then the first president of the CLC (1956), a position he held until he suffered a stroke ten years later.

For a number of years he was a member of the Executive Board of the International Confederation of Free Trade Unions (ICFTU) and the Governing Body of the International Labour Organization (ILO). In 1967 he was awarded the Order of Canada and the Centennial Medal. In the same year he was awarded an honourary doctorate by the University of New Brunswick. In 1972 he was named to the CLC Hall of Fame.

Unlike most labour leaders in Canada, Claude Jodoin did not have a "labour" background. Indeed he came from a well-to-do family, his father being solicitor for the Grand Trunk Railway. The family lived in an apartment in Montreal's Mount Royal Hotel. As a boy he attended a private school and hoped to become a surgeon. The Jodoin family were among the victims of the Great Depression, and at that point their lifestyle changed dramatically. It was then that Claude Jodoin became associated with the labour movement.

In some respects he was a complex man, not easily characterized. At times I felt he was not as secure a person as he appeared to be. Liked by all, he had no serious adversaries in the labour movement. Some have said that he was not a profound man; perhaps not, but more than anyone else in the Canadian labour movement he had the ability to harmonize divergent views. At that time in the history of Canadian labour he was unquestionably the right man in the right place.

On the evening before the final TLC convention concluded I telephoned President Jodoin asking whether I could see him briefly. He invited me to his suite where I found him reclined in a large arm chair, a drink in his hand. His face was drawn, drained of colour, and the few lines it had were furrowed deeper than usual. He seemed very tired.

In a low voice he greeted me, and pointed to the bar, offering me a drink. It was obvious that he was under some emotional strain. I refilled his glass, then poured a drink for myself and sat down. I proceeded to tell him some of the things I planned the following day. Although he was looking at me, his eyes were expressionless, his thoughts seemed elsewhere. Then, unexpectedly, he stood up and paced the floor. He turned to me with a question:

"Do you hear a lot of discussion about the merger agreement?"

"Quite a bit," I replied.

"What have you heard?"

"The same that you heard on the convention floor: most of the delegates are delighted."

He sat back in his chair, emptied his glass, and with just a trace of pensiveness spoke again:

"Yes, I know that, but when you find a man like John Bruce [a veteran member of the Plumbers' Union] and others like him, who were trade union leaders when I was still in knee pants, and who, under infinitely more difficult conditions than exist today, devoted all their lives to building this Congress, honestly believe that the merger agreement is inadequate, and that we are in fact dissolving this

Congress, and will become totally consumed by the CIO, then, dear Max, we must show some regard for their feelings, even if we believe they are mistaken."

"I agree," I said, adding, "Claude, you will recall that when John Bruce was speaking to the report of the Unity Committee, you said that the great majority of the CIO unions seceded from the TLC. Historically, that is not correct. Those unions did not secede, they were first suspended and then expelled at the 1939 TLC convention. I know that, Claude: I was there. As to your reference to dissolving the TLC, I say to you that you are, in fact, building it to become a much larger and more significant labour movement that it ever was or could be for many years if the merger did not take place."

"Yes, yes, yes," he said, somewhat impatiently.

He got up from his chair again and walked over to the window where he stood facing out and silent for a few minutes. Then, as if he had suddenly snapped out of his solemn mood, he asked me what I wanted to see him about. After our discussion, when I was about to leave, I sincerely wanted to say something to cheer him up a bit and I said:

"Claude, your place in history is solidly rooted, you may be the last President of the Trades and Labour Congress of Canada; but in a few short months you will be the first President of the Canadian Labour Congress. No one in the future will ever reach such a singular distinction."

I was glad to hear his hearty laugh as I closed the door behind me.

Claude Jodoin's closing speech the following and last day of the convention was primarily his customary expression of appreciation to people and organizations who had assisted in the convention arrangements. There was nothing remarkable about the address to that point. Then he paused, as if he were gathering his thoughts and searching for the right expression. When he began to speak again I realized at once that the thoughts about the TLC which he had expressed the previous evening were still on his mind. As the speech unfolded, all his pent-up feelings about his love for the TLC, his respect for those who were apprehensive about the merger, and his optimistic view of the future were slowly being released. I never heard him more eloquent or more impressive than he was in his closing remarks:

We have to look forward, having in mind the wonderful and great record of our TLC. We have to look forward to the fact that it will remain in the history books of our country, as well as the labour movement. We are all sentimental, we love the TLC for its accomplishments and for the aim it still has of this Congress for the future. We know, we sincerely hope, and I believe that the Canadian Congress of Labour in convention will approve amalgamation in the same spirit we have here. But the memories of the TLC, of its officers, will always be a wonderful spot in our hearts.

I now declare the 70th Annual Convention of the Trades and Labour Congress of Canada adjourned.

His gavel came down and the historic convention had ended. The TLC had passed into history.

The men and women in whose hands rested the destiny of the labour movement in Canada were, in the main, a new generation of trade unionists. They recognized fundamental trade union principles and traditions and they were also dedicated to broad social concepts, based on human values and the welfare and dignity of workers everywhere. Their vision and horizons transcended the narrow bounds of strictly trade-union traditions. The sound of that gavel was indeed a loud message to the new CLC, its leaders and members, to face the difficult challenges of an unpredictable future, irrevocably united, and to use their new-found strength with courage and wisdom.

The convention that brought about the formal merger was held at the Canadian National Exhibition in Toronto in April 1956. Several months before the convention I got in touch with Howard Conquergood, the education and welfare director of the CCL. I suggested that our two departments sponsor a joint seminar for the staff of the two congresses, prior to the merger convention. I thought such a gathering would enable the people to get to know each other better, to become friendlier, and to reduce some of the tension and ill-feeling that had developed over the years.

Conquergood liked the idea. He suggested we draft a joint memorandum to the Unity Committee seeking endorsation. We proceeded and worked out a programme. This was the first time I had met Conquergood, and it was "love at first sight" for both of us. We became very good personal friends. Howard Conquergood was a most colourful man. There was no one in the labour movement like him.

His physical appearance was not particularly uncommon, but his bulky body made him appear taller than his actual average height. His lively gray eyes vividly reflected his true nature, as well as his various needs. He was warm and compassionate, in love with humanity. He always wanted to be with people and to talk with them. His warm, effervescent disposition and his rolling, unrestrained laughter were contagious and quickly infected those with him.

He was a man of boundless energy and, despite being diabetic (which he frequently ignored in satisfying an enormous appetite), he moved about quickly and easily. He loved, more than anything else, to teach and he was an ideal labour educator. His Socratic method of teaching was always stimulating and effective. He believed that a constant dialogue between teacher and learner, and between learners themselves, was the most productive method of stimulating critical thinking, and critical thinking, he passionately believed, was the key to learning. A great deal more could and should be said about Howard Conquergood, the man and the labour educator. However, in this context it is perhaps sufficient to say that he was a distinguished pioneer in the development of labour education in Canada. His place in labour history is as secure as it is in the hearts of those privileged to know him.

The TLC-CCL Joint Staff Seminar was held at Niagara Falls in January 1956. The 138 registered participants were widely representative and far exceeded our expectations. Despite their heavy work loads, with the merger convention just three months away, the principal officers of the two congresses attended for the full week. There were also invited guests from the United States, among them John Connors, AFL-CIO Director of Education; Joe Glazer, United Rubber Workers Director of Education and an authority on labour songs; Frank McAllister, Labour Division,

Roosevelt College, Chicago; and Bill Kemsley, United Nations Office of the ICFTU.

Conquergood and I were pleasantly surprised to see the strains and hostilities that had existed between the two groups suddenly melt away as the seminar progressed. This new and welcome environment inspired us to compose a song, which we called "Unity," and which was sung to the tune of "Old Black Joe," it went:

Gone are the days
When we fought the TLC,
Gone are the days
When we both did not agree.
How did this come,
This love for the TLC?
We heard the workers' voices calling u-n-i-t-y.
We're merging,
We're merging, and the bosses they will see
We'll build a mighty union
Out of the CLC.
Gone are the days
When we fought the CCL.
Gone are the days
When we wished they'd get the bell.
How did this come
This love for the CCL?
We heard the voices calling u-n-i-t-y.
We're merging,
We're merging,
And the bosses will see,
We'll build a mighty union
Out of the CLC.

At the end of the seminar we were satisfied that our objective had been realized. In our joint report to the Unity Committee, Howard and I wrote:

It is our opinion that the seminar was eminently successful in creating a better understanding of labour's role and the staff responsibility thereto and in developing a real sense of brotherhood which will help to unify our two congresses into a united Canadian Labour Congress.

The merger agreement provided that the staffs of both congresses would be retained by the new congress; after the agreement was adopted, the Unity Committee began designating directors and field staff to the various departments. In most cases there was no difficulty. However, there was considerable disagreement when it came to designating the department of organization. Each congress wanted "their man" to head up what was considered to be the key department. The CCL people wanted their director, Joe MacKenzie, to fill the post, while I was the choice of the TLC. Gordon Cushing, who was most adamant about a TLC nominee, told me about this disagreement within the Unity Committee. He asked what I thought about the idea of having "co-directors" for the organization department.

"It won't work," I said, without hesitation.

"Why not?" he asked.

"What do you do in the event of disagreement between the co-directors?" I asked. "Some are sure to arise."

"In such cases," he answered, "both of you will discuss the matter with the executive vice-president responsible for the organization department."

"No, Gordon," I said, "It won't work. In such cases the executive vice-president would be placed in the difficult position of having to decide which of his directors was right and which was wrong. It would be like cutting the baby in half. It just won't work."

Before he could respond, I went on:

"What position does the CCL propose I should have?"

"They feel that as you are the TLC director of organization and education, you should retain the post of education director, and that Joe Mackenzie should retain organization. In that way both of you would be treated equally."

I thought for a few minutes, and then said:

"You know Gordon, their position seems both reasonable and logical to me."

"What do you mean?" he asked, obviously not having expected such a comment.

"I don't think it makes much difference. I'd be just as happy with either of the positions," I replied.

He seemed a bit more relaxed and, I suspected, relieved, because he honestly thought I would be distressed if I were not given the organization department. I have never regretted the decision, for it added a new and broader dimension to my life, with many exciting opportunities and rewarding experiences.

The Unity Committee also decided that Howard Conquergood would be the Ontario director of education and move from his national office at Ottawa to the regional office in Toronto. At the same time it was decided that Henry Weisbach, who was then on the CCL staff at Toronto, would be offered the opportunity to move to Ottawa to head up the CLC's Political Education Department.

In my opinion this was an unfair and bad decision. After all, I thought, Conquergood was already a CCL national director, and since a new national position was to be filled he should receive it, rather than being demoted to a provincial position. On the other hand, if Weisbach was assigned to the CLC's regional director of organization, there would be no change in his status. I told Cushing what I thought. He said the CCL had made the recommendation, and since it involved CCL personnel the TLC had raised no objection. I asked whether the decision was irreversible. What if Weisbach was not too keen about moving to Ottawa and what if Conquergood was keen on heading up the political education department, remaining at the national office? Cushing, with some caution, said he saw no reason why the committee would not reverse its decision. I was satisfied with that.

I then arranged to meet with Weisbach, on the pretext of discussing a number of matters, though in reality I wanted to know how he felt about his new assignment. My suspicion proved correct. He said that he naturally felt honoured at being assigned to such an important post, but both he and his wife were a bit apprehensive about moving to Ottawa.

"Max," he said, in his usual frank and honest manner, "Believe me, I am very happy here in Toronto, and I would gladly take a provincial position if it were offered to me."

"Would you be willing to switch posts with Howard and head the education department in Ontario?" I asked.

"I'd be glad to make the change," he replied, without a moment's hesitation.

I said I would speak to Conquergood, and if he agreed to the switch, which I was sure he would be delighted to do, then they might both make such a recommendation to the Unity Committee; and that is what happened. Weisbach remained as the Ontario Director of Education until he joined the staff of the Ontario Federation of Labour in 1962. Conquergood remained in his post until his untimely death in 1958. Both men served the labour movement with great sincerity and distinction.

CHAPTER SEVEN
Labour Education

I WORKED IN THE FIELD of labour education from 1952 to 1977. In that quarter century I had my opportunities to speak and write about labour education, as well as learning about the wide-ranging aspects of the subject, and forming some definite opinions.

There is no comprehensive definition of labour education that is fully acceptable to all. Differences arise, not only with respect to its scope, objectives, and methods, but also with regard to the immediate aims and the long-term goals. In large measure a union's educational programme reflects not only its conception of the labour movement, but also its attitude toward society and life itself. If, as in some cases, the labour movement is regarded only as a force designed to protect workers against abuse, to strive constantly for improved economic conditions, and to counter-balance the power of management, then the educational programme of that union will, in the main, stress the training of competent union technicians and administrators.

But if, in addition, the labour movement is regarded as a social force dedicated to the attainment of a better society, a richer and fuller life for all, and an interdependent world in lasting peace, then the programme of that union will include studies of a wider dimension.

Prior to the merger both congresses had labour education programmes. In 1951 the CCL had appointed Howard Conquergood as its first full-time official in charge of education, and he had begun to develop a nation-wide programme. In the TLC, before my appointment as national director of organization and education in 1952, educational activities had been a matter of local initiative. The provincial federations of labour in the four western provinces, a number of district trades and labour councils, and several of the larger unions had education committees that periodically organized weekend schools. These generally dealt with traditional trade union "tool" subjects — union administration, shop stewards' duties, parliamentary procedure, and collective bargaining. Some unions participated in programmes sponsored by universities, the Workers' Education Association, or the Canadian Association for Adult Education (CAAE).

There were exceptions, the most notable of which was the extensive programme conducted by the ILGWU in Montreal. In the late 1940s that union had a broad educational programme covering the following subjects:

Language There were three classes in English and one in French, each with twenty-five sessions, to assist members, including New Canadians, to acquire and improve language skills.

Vocations Courses were available to help workers upgrade their skills; particularly for cutters, one of the most highly-skilled crafts.

Trade Unionism A course providing a broad introduction to the history, objectives, and activities of trade unions generally and the ILGWU in particular.

Recreation and Culture In the ILGWU such activities date back many years, in both Canada and the United States. In Montreal they included drama, singing, dancing, softball, and bowling.

Displaced Persons In addition to the language courses, open forums were held once a week for New Canadians with lectures and discussions on the history, geography, and resources of Canada, as well as on current events, the practice of democracy and similar general subjects.

These courses proved very popular, and many union members took part.

When I first assumed my new post at TLC headquarters, I began to prepare an outline covering the role and responsibilities of my department. There was no difficulty identifying the nature of our involvement in organizational activities, but I had considerable difficulty outlining, in practical terms, the role and scope of the Congress in the field of education. There were several reasons. First, I had no previous experience in designing a nation-wide educational programme. Secondly, I had only fragmentary knowledge of what other unions were doing in this area. Thirdly, my knowledge of the technical aspects of teaching adults was very limited, to say the least.

I set out to learn as much as I could in the shortest possible time. As there was practically no educational material available at the TLC headquarters, I wrote several American colleagues. Among them were John Connors, Educational Director of the AFL; Mark Starr, Educational Director of the ILGWU; and Dr. Otto Pragan, Educational Director of the International Chemical Workers' Union. I asked them for material, including programmes and course outlines. They responded quickly, sending me a mass of literature that was most useful.

Then I met with Roby Kidd, the Director of the CAAE, and I asked for his assistance and guidance in designing and developing an educational programme for the TLC. He was delighted to held me.

Dr. James Robbins Kidd, affectionately called "Roby" the world over, was a remarkable person. He was more, much more, than a competent educator; he was an effective leader, a willing and helpful advisor, a man possessed of a deep and compassionate philosophy and with a boundless faith and love for all. I first met him in the mid-1940s, and for almost 40 years I held a deep affection for him. Through those many years we worked together on many national and some international projects. His intellectual excellence, his concentrated and undivided attention when he was listening to a problem, his views, and advice, expressed so simply, with kindness and humility, were always a rewarding and emotional experience.

When Roby Kidd died on 21 March 1982, adult education throughout the world lost a singular and monumental teacher, philosopher, and humanist. I feel honoured and privileged to have known and worked with him, and to have had him as a friend for 40 years. Among the many tributes paid him, few express more eloquently the kind of man he was then do the words of Nancy Cochrane, one of his students in 1981:

To Roby:
Sir, you are my teacher
An ageless wonder of man,
In wisdom, in love, in full stature
Humbly living your life-long task
of learning and giving to us all,
The world over ...

When I first went seeking his help we began to take inventory of labour educational programmes in unions, the universities, and various organizations. Going frequently to his crowded files and shelves, laden with books and magazines, he began meticulously listing the names of the institutions and their programmes. Often he would make some interesting comment about a particular organization or programme. I was very impressed, indeed overwhelmed, with the breadth of his knowledge and understanding of labour education.

At our second meeting we discussed the role of the Congress in promoting a sustained programme. His advice and assistance in identifying guidelines for designing specific programmes for union members at various levels of responsibility were invaluable.

At that time, when I moved to Ottawa, there was at least one TLC organizer in every province. As in my case, their main responsibility was to organize and service unions. This they did very well, needing little guidance from me. However, in labour education the situation was somewhat different, and the organizers were expected to initiate educational programmes in their area. Because none of us was a trained labour educator, we relied on each other for ideas, advice, and assistance. Our interdependence resulted in a close-knit group of colleagues and good friends.

Our first co-ordinated effort was to encourage provincial federations and district trades and labour councils to establish educational committees where none existed. It was intended that these committees would plan and conduct programmes with the local TLC organizer acting as co-ordinator. In 1954 I was able to report to the TLC Executive Council that all the federations and many of the councils had established committees and were conducting programmes.

In my travels across the country I met with these committees to review and assist in their plans. Every programme was self-sustaining; the unions did not ask for, nor did they expect, the TLC to provide funds. In fact, in the early days, my department had no designated budget. The Congress assistance was in the main advisory, with the active involvement of TLC representatives in the area.

With few exceptions, the programmes were held on weekends, generally with two or three tool courses. They were very popular, attracting as many as 100 to a class. In most cases the instructors were officers of affiliated unions, who were always happy and willing to co-operate. In addition, the Congress worked with the provincial federations in British Columbia and Alberta in planning one-week winter schools at Parkdale, B.C., and at the Banff School of Fine Arts. As well as tool courses, these winter schools provided studies in elementary economics, industrial relations, collective bargaining, labour law, and international affairs. The instructors were recruited from universities and government departments, as well as from the labour movement. By 1955 similar one-week schools were being conducted in most provinces.

Although our members participated in increasing numbers, the overall programme suffered from some serious weaknesses. Most of our instructors knew very little about teaching methods and techniques. In many cases the level of instruction was too elementary for some and too advanced for others. Except for the Shop Steward's Manual, which I had prepared, we had no printed or visual material. In an attempt to overcome these difficulties, at least to some extent, we worked with the CAAE in organizing several instructors' training courses.

We also began, where possible, to separate the participants into elementary and advanced classes. Getting additional education material relevant to the subjects was more difficult. We asked for, and received, material from the ILO, the AFL, and the International Confederation of Free Trade Unions (ICFTU), as well as from some unions. We also began to prepare and print some material of our own. The excellent films produced by the National Film Board were of great value and were frequently used for instruction and as the basis of discussion.

At the time of the merger of the two congresses in 1956, the TLC field staff consisted of twenty full-time representatives, doing both organizational and educational work.

After the merger, our educational programme assumed a much broader perspective, dealing with such subjects as political action, economics, international affairs, co-operative housing, health and welfare, and so on. Concern with broader social issues increased as the labour movement faced more difficult and complex problems.

The resolution on education adopted at the founding convention of the CLC read in part:

The CLC has embarked on a broad union educational programme designed to equip union members for more effective participation in all aspects of unionism, in its problems, its practices, and its policies; and with a better understanding of this past history, its present position, and its future aims."

This generally reflected my own view of what labour education is all about.

Shortly after the founding convention, the CLC officers asked the directors of all departments to submit programme proposals. I wanted to submit something more than a chronological list of proposed events and topics. I wanted my contribution to be a thoughtful statement encompassing what I believed to be the philosophy, the social concepts, and the objectives of the trade union movement — a statement that would serve as a framework within which the scope and substance of labour education would be clearly identified.

I produced the following document:

The aim of education in the labour movement is first to stimulate and create a fundamental understanding of our society. It considers and analyzes the dynamics of our industrial democracy generally, and the labour movement in particular. It stresses the philosophy and the social, economic, and political objectives of organized labour. Second, it is designed to instruct and train union members in methods that will enable them to discharge their union responsibilities more efficiently and help them play a more important role in the labour movement.

Labour education is, and must be, purposeful. It is not, and should not be, abstract and dogmatic. It should stress the importance of the labour movement as an integral part of our democratic society. Its experience and knowledge, its increasing strength and growing social influence must be geared to measures that are in the best interest of the community as a whole, and compatible with our democratic way of life.

The scope of labour education is wide, and is constantly widening to the same proportion that social, economic and political issues arise and multiply. A meaningful programme of labour education encompasses the sum total of labour's activities — its immediate objectives, its long-range goals and aspirations.

The officers accepted this introductory statement without change. The organizational structure within which the major part of this programme was to be conducted was:

Institutes Generally weekend courses for local union officers and members designed to provide broad trade union education, but more particularly training in methods and procedures in local union administration, collective bargaining, grievance procedure and similar "tool" subjects. The courses were to be conducted on two levels, basic and advanced.

Summer and Winter Schools Courses of longer duration, in most cases a week or more. Such schools to be designed primarily for members with previous labour education experience. The courses, although similar to those in the institutes, would be more detailed and more concentrated.

Staff Seminars In most cases of one-week duration, designed primarily for full-time staff personnel. Advanced studies in current social, economic, political, and organizational problems of concern to the labour movement.

Industry Schools Short programmes conducted jointly by the CLC Education Department and a union, with the courses specifically directed to the particular industry and union.

Our programme across the country developed rapidly. From the time of the founding convention in 1956 to December 1957 we conducted 160 schools in which 14,000 union members participated. In the following period, 1958-1959, the number of schools increased to 303, with an attendance of well over 23,000. At these schools there was an average of five different courses; thus a total of 1,500 courses was given. We estimated that about 300 instructors, all of whom came from the labour movement and at their own union's expense, took part. Union officers seldom, if ever, turned down a request to lecture at educational functions. This remarkable co-operation between the Congress and its affiliates was the key to the systematic growth of the programme and the rapid development of labour education in Canada.

The school records showed a substantial turnover of participants, ranging from 40 to 80 per cent. Although the number of participants continued to increase impressively, they still represented only about 2 per cent of the CLC membership.

In order to increase this participation rate we encouraged and assisted in the formation of education committees in provincial federations, trades and labour councils, and local unions. At the CLC convention in April 1960, I reported:

> All Federations of Labour and most Trades and Labour Councils have established education committees. Regional Directors of Education have also helped to establish such committees in many local unions, and have assisted them in developing their own education programmes.

We considered such assistance to be an important element in the work of the department. The programme was, of course, not without problems and shortcomings, some of which were:

1) a shortage of well-qualified teachers;
2) the lack of clearly defined and planned programmes of progression from one level to another;
3) a failure to widen the scope of our programme by including subjects additional to the "tool" courses;
4) the lack of audio-visual and printed educational material.

We initiated a number of measures in the hope of overcoming these problems, to some extent at least. Roby Kidd assisted in constructing a national programme for the training of teachers. Beginning in 1961 a number of such courses, as well as refresher courses for those with some teaching experience, were conducted in all regions. Although the problem of recruiting well-qualified instructors was not completely solved, a number of new people were involved, and others improved their teaching skills.

Steadily we began to broaden the horizon of our programme by introducing a variety of course in the humanities and social sciences. We referred to these as "liberal education," which, for our purpose, meant studies other than "tool" subjects.

The department listed 40 course descriptions. About half were regarded as "tool" subjects and the others as "liberal." For example, there were two courses offered in collective bargaining — "Aspects of Collective Bargaining" and "The Role of Collective Bargaining in a Democratic Society." The first, "Aspects of Collective Bargaining," was treated as a "tool" course, covering progressively studies in "The Meaning of Collective Bargaining," "Preparation for Collective Bargaining," "Methods and Skills in Collective Bargaining," "Trends in Collective Bargaining," "Analyzing and Drafting Collective Agreements," and "The Law and Collective Bargaining." These approaches were intended to improve the skills and efficiency of union officers and members of bargaining committees. The other course, "The Role of Collective Bargaining in a Democratic Society," had a different but related purpose. There the intent was to improve the general knowledge of members by analyzing the essential components of society (labour, management, the mass media, and government), and relating them to the economy and the collective bargaining process.

The same principle applied to studies in the general field of economics. "Tool" subjects were concerned with wages and wage demands, pension plans, holidays, vacations, and similar subjects directly related to the economic and social welfare of the worker and his family. The "liberal" subjects in this area had a different, but no less important, objective. These studies were intended to assist the members to understand better the structure of the national economy: how it works, the relationship between wages, prices, productivity, inflation, unemployment, alternative systems, and the interdependence of world economies.

It may be asked, which has the greater priority and which is more important — "tool" courses or "liberal" studies? My reply would be that they are of equal importance, and the priorities are determined by the needs and interests of the participating students.

For a group of stewards interested in learning how best to handle shop problems, specific "tool" subjects, such as "Grievance Procedure" or "Know Your Contract," might well have top priority. But, for union members with no specific union responsibility, and therefore no immediate need for a "tool" course, it might well be that their interest, and therefore their priority, would go to a "liberal" subject, such as "The History of the Labour Movement," "What Collective Bargaining is About," or "Unions in Society." Full-time officers would generally attend seminars dealing with broad economic, political, or organizational problems. Thus, priorities are determined by the interests, needs, and responsibilities of the participants.

There are some in the labour movement who argue that the primary and only aim of education undertaken by unions should be to train members to be more efficient in discharging their particular union responsibilities. They may agree that "liberal education" is very useful, but feel that universities, colleges, and similar institutions could offer such courses more objectively and better designed than those conducted by the labour movement itself.

There is, unquestionably, a useful and positive place that universities can, and indeed do, play in the field of labour education, which I will discuss later. I also agree that in some cases university courses may very well be better designed, but I am not overly impressed with the degree of "objectivity" in some university courses on trade union issues. Moreover, I do not hold the view that labour education, in broad terms, can or should realistically be so absolutely objective as to be without a degree of trade union bias.

If labour education should, as I believe, encompass a wide range of organizational needs and social issues, then the labour movement, where possible in co-operation with universities and others, must develop, conduct, and ensure that such programmes reflect its concerns and policies. It cannot sub-contract out its institutional interests and responsibilities.

Labour education, *per se*, is not a panacea for solving of all union problems. The knowledge and the skills that a union member acquires through education are tools, as much as the plough is the tool of the farmer, the hammer of the carpenter, and the scalpel of the surgeon. But, if the farmer, carpenter, or surgeon is to do his job well, he must have strong and steady hands and use his tool with care, responsibility, and wisdom.

I hold firmly to my views on labour education. However, some labour educators, particularly in the United States, thought I was overstressing the importance and urgency of introducing "liberal" subjects into our programme in the late 1950s. They argued that other union needs were much greater. Union membership in both Canada and the United States was growing rapidly, and they felt the immediate need was the training of thousands of union officers. "Liberal" subjects, they said, could be introduced later, when more resources were available for education.

These divergent views surfaced in a rather spirited fashion in a discussion between some Canadians, myself included, and some American labour educators at the first Joint Conference of Directors of Education, held at Washington, D.C., in January 1959. Essentially, our disagreement was not on the substance of labour education but rather on priorities and timing. Those of us who debated the issue reflected the views of our respective labour movements. And so, with some exceptions, the United Auto Workers and the United Steelworkers being the main ones, labour education in the United States proceeded on the path of pragmatic bread-and-butter issues, while in Canada it was on a broader base, including social, economic, political, and international issues.

CHAPTER EIGHT

The International Spirit

THE SCOPE OF OUR ACTIVITIES in the international field expanded rapidly following the merger. From the time I first attended an International Labour Organization (ILO) conference at Geneva in 1952, I had become increasingly convinced of the importance of Canadian educational officials establishing links with their counterparts in other countries. This opportunity for the labour movement in Canada has seldom, if ever, been illustrated so clearly as it was in the Banff International Seminar of 1957.

The International Confederation of Free Trade Unions (ICFTU) and its Latin division (ORIT) readily accepted our invitation to co-operate in sponsoring the seminar. William Kensley, the ICFTU representative at the United Nations, was designated to work with us in directing the programme.

The theme was the interdependence of the economically-developed countries and the underdeveloped countries. Seventy-five delegates from 30 countries took part. The countries represented were: Argentina, Aruba, Austria, Barbados, Canada, Chile, Colombia, Costa Rice, Cuba, El Salvador, Ghana, Guatemala, Haiti, India, Italy, Jamaica, Malaya, Mexico, Nigeria, Pakistan, Peru, Poland (in exile), Singapore, Spain (in exile), Sweden, Trinidad, Tunisia, Uruguay, United States, and Venezuela (in exile).

The sessions at the Banff School of Fine Arts were intense and sometimes spirited. Although a great deal of attention was naturally given to trade union matters, there was also considerable discussion and emphasis on broad issues of understanding among the people of all the countries represented.

The seminar commenced at Banff, where most of the formal sessions were held. The programme continued in Toronto and concluded in Montreal. All this obviously required a great deal of effort in establishing an effective organization. The complex arrangements and services required were efficiently provided and carried out by a number of dedicated trade unionists across the country.

Bill Kemsley and I readily agreed on our respective responsibilities; generally he would guide the substance of the programme, and I would oversee the organizational arrangements. All the proceedings were simultaneously translated by one of three professional English-Spanish translators who were brought from Mexico. Gordon Wilkinson, the CLC Regional Director of Education, directed the office staff of three English and two Spanish secretaries, who often worked far into the night to cope with the volume of work.

Gower Markle, Educational Director of the United Steelworkers, and Bert Hepworth, Educational Director of the Canadian Brotherhood of Railway Employees, were in charge of the preparation of daily resumés of lectures and discussions. These were prepared in both English and Spanish, mimeographed and distributed to the students daily. This was greatly appreciated. Bob Smeal of the British Columbia Federation of Labour was responsible for tape recording all the proceed-

ings. Joe Miyazawa, Education and Research Director for the International Wood-
workers, looked after a multitude of details connected with transportation and
solved many problems in a most efficient manner.

During the time that I was CLC Director of Education I knew of no labour
education seminar that received wider press coverage. Jack Williams, Public
Relations Director of the CLC, was in charge of publicity. Part of his report read:

A staff representative of The Canadian Press, which serves all Canadian dailies, the
majority of radio stations, and the CBC, and which feeds Canadian news to the Associated
Press and Reuters had a staff man at Banff for the first four days and another for the last
three days. We took a press clipping service and to date we have received 185 clippings from
Canadian dailies. They are still coming in and do not include any quantity of clippings of
stories carried when students made post-Banff visits to various centres. Undoubtedly these
visits resulted in local coverage. From Banff we issued twelve general press releases on
particular talks or discussions. In addition, background sheets were prepared on: (1) the
Seminar in general; (2) the Vancouver programme on the arrival of the group from Latin
America; (3) the Toronto visit; and (4) the Montreal visit. Our mailing list for press releases
was 214, including some twenty-three papers to which students requested mailing, and some
twenty foreign correspondents located in New York.

At the outset of the Seminar a Students' Council was elected, consisting of nine representatives from various countries. Wesley Wainright, Jamaica, Paul Koch, Austria, and Timothy
Ogum, Ghana, were responsible for the publication of a daily bulletin which reflected the
activities of the day and published announcements. The bulletin was usually distributed at
breakfast and was read with both interest and amusement. The Students' Council was
responsible for all social activities and also dealt with personal problems that arose from
time to time.

Funding the Seminar presented difficulties. There were problems raising the necessary
funds from the labour movement in Canada, and, as this was our first such effort, we had
difficulty establishing a projected cost. In addition, we were not sure what the response of
our unions would be. We anticipated that participants from Europe would be financed by
their own organizations, but we knew that participants from Latin America and the Caribbean, as well as from Asia and Africa, would have to be fully subsidized. As best as we were
able, we estimated the cost of their transportation, their two week stay at Banff, transportation
to eastern Canada, and the overall cost of the seminar.

Our plans to raise the required finances included various methods. First, a general appeal
for contributions was sent to all provincial federations, labour councils, and individual
unions. Secondly, an approach to some of the larger unions asking them to finance one or
more scholarships for a trade unionist employed in their industry, or one similar, in Asia,
Africa, Latin America, or the Caribbean. We were very pleased with the number of unions
that accepted what one union officer called "an innovative suggestion." Thirdly, we requested contributions from the ICFTU and the ILO.

The overall response to our financial appeal from Canadian unions was most
gratifying, indeed we over-subscribed our estimated requirement. In my report to
the CLC Executive Council, I stated:

It will be noted that, with the exception of the ILO and ICFTU contributions of $5,000 each, the balance was raised in Canada. After paying all expenses and making allowance for outstanding commitments, there is still a balance. Brother Bill Kemsley and I recommend that this amount go to the ICFTU Solidarity Fund, designated for educational purposes, and more particularly for future ICFTU International Seminars.

The first three days at Banff were devoted to an examination of the state of trade unions in various countries. Bell Kemsley led off with a review of the global scene. John Connor of the AFL-CIO and Ralph Showalter of the United Auto Workers reviewed the situation in the United States. Bert Hepworth and I reported on the Canadian scene.

The trade union situation in Latin America and the Caribbean, as well as the social, economic, and political complexities of the region, were reviewed by Ricardo Temoche, Director of the Trade Union School at Lima, Peru, and Manuel Mendez, Education Director of ORIT. Ken Sterling of Jamaica also spoke on the situation in the Caribbean. Paul Koch of Austria and M. Massetti of Italy, with Bertel Broms of Sweden, led the discussion on the European situation. J.C. Dixit, India, and S.M. Zafar, Pakistan, spoke on the situation in Asia. Timothy Ogum, Ghana, and Michael Labinjo, Nigeria, discussed the African situation.

Among the seminar participants were several who were living in exile because of the opposition of their governments to the free trade union movement. Roman Stefanowski and Edward Glowacki spoke of the Polish trade unions in exile, and Pedro Velex on behalf of the Spanish trade unions.

Economic assistance to Third World countries was naturally a high-priority subject, and leading the discussion were three well-qualified speakers: Nik Cavell, Canadian administrator of the Colombo Plan, Dr. Edgar McInnis, president of the Canadian Institute of International Affairs, and Philip Stuchen, an economist with the Department of Trade and Commerce. The speakers said that Canada was well aware of the urgent need for increased support for underdeveloped countries. Stuchen stressed the fact that social stability in many countries depended on the kind and amount of assistance they received. McInnis spoke particularly of the situation in Africa, south of the Sahara. He said there was a great need for everything: capital, education, markets for both raw materials and manufactured goods, communications, public health education, and hydro power.

Nik Cavell read a paper on wide ranging problems in Asia. He argued:

The needs of the whole area are so colossal, the wants of the people so many and varied, that one can only hope in a short presentation to mention some of the most obvious. We must remember the recent history of most of Asia. Great changes have taken place in the last few years. In India, Pakistan, Ceylon, Burma, Indonesia, and the French Indies strong national-istic movements fought for freedom from the colonial powers then governing them.

When, eventually, freedom was obtained these nationalist — and in many cases revolu-tionary — movements had to be turned into responsible administrations. Unfortunately, what makes a successful revolutionary movement is unlikely to make a settled day-to-day administration; and in many of these countries the sorting out process is not yet by any means over. This results in the instability in government of which we find so many examples in the South-East Asia area. In some of these countries satisfactory constitutions have not yet evolved. It is also not unnatural that leaders of revolutionary movements should themselves find it a little difficult to settle down as really democratic Prime Ministers.

The discussion that followed these three presentations evoked some pointed comments, particularly from foreign participants. Some said they were fully familiar with the complexities and hardships in their own area, but they were anxious to know what plans Canada, and other western nations, had for extending greater economic assistance to the poor nations. Other delegates agreed, arguing, rather delicately, that their countries were poor because of centuries of colonial rule. One participant took exception to Cavell's remark about revolutionary leaders finding it "a little difficult to settle down as really democratic Prime Ministers." I thought this participant misunderstood Cavell's observation. However, I also believed Cavell underestimated the sensitiveness of some foreign participants to even the mildest form of criticism of their leaders.

Discussion on this subject, together with the previous three days examination of the trade union situation in various countries, was very revealing and productive. It enabled all of us to know much better the world we were living in and to appreciate better the vital necessity of recognizing global inter-dependence.

The three top-ranking officers of the Canadian Labour Congress visited the seminar. President Claude Jodoin formally welcomed the visitors to Canada. He referred to the new spirit of unity, established in the trade union movement in Canada through the merger which had taken place the previous year. He also spoke of the possibilities and responsibilities of the newly-created CLC, and gave assurance that international relations would be high on the CLC's agenda.

Secretary-Treasurer Donald MacDonald declared that the CLC fully supported the ICFTU's stated purpose of "bread, peace, and freedom for all." He said those who believed in these principles should work for their fulfillment through the international trade union movement.

Executive Vice-President Gordon Cushing outlined the wide range of CLC representation on various boards and commissions as well as private institutions. He emphasized the importance the CLC placed on education. Other speakers from universities, governments, and trade unions dealt with various aspects of the world's problems: the growth in population, agricultural difficulties, the growing imbalance between the rich and the poor nations, and the increasing East-West tension with all its ominous possibilities.

But, of all the numerous speakers who addressed the Seminar, none attracted the public attention given Charles Millard, the ICFTU's Director of Organization. Millard was a Canadian trade unionist with a distinguished record. He had been prominently involved in the earliest days of the United Auto Workers in Canada and was one of the founders of the United Steelworkers, becoming Canadian Director of that union. In 1956 he had resigned from that position to work with the ICFTU on a world-wide basis. Throughout his career he had been extremely active politically. Not only was he one of the most ardent advocates of direct political action by unions in Canada, but he became personally involved, serving two terms in the Ontario Legislature as a member of the Co-operative Commonwealth

Federation (CCF), the forerunner of the NDP.

The part of his address to the Seminar that created what came to be known as "The Charlie Millard Affair" dealt with unions and politics. In retrospect it may be regarded as "a tempest in a teapot," but, because of Millard's status, it caused quite a stir at the time. The misinterpretation of his remarks demonstrated the complexities of union-political relationships, particularly under the varied conditions prevailing in some countries and confronting fledgling unions.

In the course of his presentation, Millard said:

> The labour movement must be independent and responsible only to its membership. Labour unions must not permit themselves to be used or exploited by political parties, nor should unions permit paternalism from governments or employers. Unscrupulous politicians must not be permitted to use unions as tools for their personal ambitions. Unions, however, must take political action and make independent demands on political parties and governments.

The following day newspapers across the country gave prominence to reports of the address, suggesting that Millard was advising the trade union movement in Canada to steer clear of endorsing a political party, a position completely at variance with that of a large part of the union movement in Canada, and to the cause to which Millard had personally contributed so much.

The *Calgary Herald*, for example, headed their report: "Politics Out for Unions." The account went on to say that Millard had warned of "the danger of unions becoming too closely tied to political parties." Moreover, it said, Millard in a subsequent interview had gone still further and had suggested that, perhaps, the time had come for Canadian labour to stop automatically supporting the CCF.

This was a complete misrepresentation of his remarks, and MIllard wrote *The Canadian Press*, which had distributed the report, complaining that it had given "a completely distorted impression of what I had actually said." He pointed out that two-thirds of the students at the Seminar were "from unions in their infancy, a good many struggling for their very existence." He said he had told the Seminar that political action was "a must for trade unions," but the form such action should take "must be made by the unions themselves, not imposed by a political party, or a government or any outside agency." He said further that he had warned of "paper unions," created by politicians "on the make," and of paternalistic relations between unions, political parties, and governments. As far as the Canadian situation was concerned, he said he saw no reason to change the position he had followed consistently for twenty years.

The "Millard Affair" pointed up the problems faced by many trade unionists in developing countries. Millard's well-known views on political action by unions were also the views and principles of all free trade union movements in the western democratic countries. However, not all unions, regardless of their association with the ICFTU, functioned in democratic societies. In the more than seven years that I worked for the ILO in Asia, I found that in one country every major political party had its own trade union centre. In another country, the full-time president of the

Union federation was on the company payroll, paid the salary he had received before he became president. In still another country, the government built a large modern headquarters for the national trade union congress. And in another small country the government provided funds to the union so that it could function well.

In such cases it would be naive, I believe, to say that the governments or political parties did not exercise some degree of influence and control over the affairs of the trade union movement. Yet some Asian union officers argued that without some government support they could not maintain their organizations. In reality, in some Third World countries, the temptation for unions to accept outside support transcends the principle of independence and free trade unionism, as it is understood by unions in democratic countries.

Today, government assistance to some trade union activities, such as education, is accepted, but when government assistance becomes dependent on labour support for government policies, then the labour movement becomes subservient to the government, and by degrees loses its independence and social usefulness.

That, I believe, is what Millard was talking about.

At the conclusion of the Banff programme three buses carried the students to Calgary, from where they dispersed for several days to industrial centres in the east. There they stayed in the homes of Canadian workers, many being guests of unions that had sponsored their scholarship. Local labour councils arranged programmes that included visits to industries, attending union meetings, giving press interviews, and in, at least one case, walking a picket line.

Many students later reported that these visits were one of the highlights of their Canadian experience. Although at times language was somewhat of a problem, it was never a barrier to the spontaneous friendship that quickly developed with their union brothers and sisters. It was an equally happy experience for their hosts, with whom a number of students later carried on correspondence.

After the buses left Banff, my wife and I, with several maintenance employees, were the only occupants of the school. That afternoon I walked aimlessly toward the auditorium where the Seminar had been held. As I entered I saw the rows of tables with small, colourful national flags beside the printed cards that identified the participants. At the rear was the stage from which panelists and other speakers had addressed the students. On the walls hung bright banners with popular union slogans printed in bold red and black letters.

Alone in that desolate silence, I became absorbed in pleasant memories of the previous two weeks. Soon I became engulfed in strangely mixed feelings, satisfied with the success of the seminar, yet a little sad that it had ended. Working with such dedicated people had been a happy experience. From the moment the first group from Latin America set foot in Vancouver, we had enjoyed a high degree of co-operation from fellow trade unionists across the country. At Vancouver they had been greeted by Percy Bengough, as honorary president of the CLC. The British Columbia Federation of Labour and the Vancouver and District Labour Council were gracious hosts for three days, taking the visitors on tours of the city and visits to industrial establishments.

The day after the departure of the students from Banff we left for Toronto, where the group reassembled. The first day of the Toronto programme was an open-house session with trade unionists from the area invited to visit with the seminar students. On the second day the students reported on their experiences in visiting Canadian homes and industries. That evening they were entertained at a banquet given by the federal government, with Labour Minister Michael Starr as the main speaker.

On 29 September the group moved to Montreal, where they were guests at a dinner given by the City of Montreal. CLC Vice-President Roger Provost, a member of the Montreal Municipal Council, presided. They were also entertained at a luncheon given by the Jewish Labour Committee.

Then, on 1 October, the foreign students left Canada, flying in many directions to many countries. They took with them a new understanding and appreciation of the solidarity of the trade union movement, in a truly international sense, and they left their Canadian brothers and sisters with new insights into that phenomenon.

CHAPTER NINE
The Broader Involvement

BEYOND OUR IMMEDIATE CONCERNS within the labour movement, our department
became increasingly involved in a number of peripheral areas related to labour's
interests. This list of committees and organizations on which I represented the
Congress was impressive. It included: CLC Educational Committee, National
Vocational Training and Apprenticeship Committee, Co-operative Labour Committee, Human Rights Committee, Trade Union Film Committee, Frontier College,
and the Canadian Association for Adult Education.

An example of this type of activity was my participation in the National
Apprenticeship Council, a federal government body. In the course of attending
meetings I developed firm opinions about vocational and technical training. In an
address at Windsor, Ontario, I expressed some of these views.

Canadian law prescribed that an apprentice in the construction industry had to
have four years of training before he could be regarded as a journeyman or a
fully-qualified tradesman. I regarded this as antiquated and ridiculous. It did not
require four years of training to become a qualified painter, plasterer, or bricklayer,
especially taking into consideration modern materials and methods. Beyond this,
I suggested that training skills in related crafts was both possible and desirable.

The law also required apprentices to complete the four years of training by the
time they were 21. I had visited the Kingston Penitentiary and had talked to young
prisoners of 19 and 20 who were being trained for construction. They were about
to be released, but there was no way they could meet this age requirement, and so
the training they had received was of little or no value.

The *Toronto Globe and Mail* carried an account of my address under a
four-column heading: "Current Technical Education Said Outdated By Union
Official." The article recited my criticisms, particularly my objection to the age
limit on apprenticeship and my support for training in multiple, but reasonably
related, trades.

Then all hell broke loose at CLC headquarters. President Jodoin hurriedly
summoned me to his office. Highly agitated, he handed me a telegram from John
Bruce, Canadian Vice-President of the Plumbers' International Union and a leading
spokesman for the building trades unions. It was a blistering cable. Bruce strongly
objected to a Congress employee speaking publicly on building trades matters
without prior consultation with the unions involved. He said I should be reprimanded for my "unwarranted observations on our crafts."

I told the President I was sorry and that I had had no intention of harming the
construction unions, nor embarrassing the Congress. I pointed out that what I had
said was a repetition of what he, the President, had said previously at an ILO
conference at Geneva. He snapped back that he had made that statement on my
advice. He walked over to where I was sitting; a big man he towered over me.
Gently, he put his hand on my shoulder, then with a smile he said: "My dear Max,

what I said, I said in Geneva, not in Windsor."

I left his office both confused and amused, and I heard no more of the affair. It did, I think, demonstrate, however, the complex position of the national Congress, representing so many varied interests.

A number of our outside interests were related to education. In Canada, organized labour's interest and concern in education had never been restricted to in-union programmes, but has extended to education in its broadest sense, and has recognized the opportunities presented by co-operation with other educational bodies. When I met with Dr. Roby Kidd in summer 1956, seeking his advice and assistance, we discussed the role which Canadian universities could, and should, play in our programme.

At that time several universities were conducting short courses on broad labour subjects in which union members participated. These included: the University of British Columbia, the Manitoba Labour Institute at the University of Manitoba, the University of Toronto at Ajax, Laval University in Quebec, and St. Francis Xavier and Dalhousie universities in Nova Scotia.

Although there were variations in the structure and quality of these programmes, co-operation between labour and universities had been going on for some time.

In 1956 we wanted to expand and enhance that co-operation, and we felt some form of systematic liaison would be helpful. As a first step we agreed on a national conference, sponsored by the CLC and the CAAE. Gordon Hawkins, associate director of the CAAE, was made responsible for organizing the conference.

The first National University-Labour Conference on Education and Co-operation was held at Ottawa 15-17 December 1956, about six months after the merger. The response was larger and more representative than we had anticipated, with a total of 111 delegates representing universities, the Canadian and Catholic Confederation of Labour, government departments, and the mass media, as well as the CLC and its unions.

Speakers at the opening session were Gordon Cushing, Executive Vice-President of the CLC; Gordon Hawkins; Dean G.F. Curtis, University of British Columbia; and myself. I emphasized that, for university-labour co-operation to be realistic, labour's participation had to be something more than a name on a letterhead, as it had been in some previous instances. We were concerned with active participation in planning and establishing a continuing relationship. Following a panel discussion on the points raised in the opening addresses, the delegates divided into three study groups examining union education and the mass media, union education and government departments, as well as union education and the universities.

The most significant contribution to continued and improved labour-university co-operation came in a resolution which read:

Be it resolved that this conference establish a continuing committee with membership from the universities, organized labour, and the Canadian Association for Adult Education. The purposes to be:

1) To act as a clearing house.

2) To consult with local or regional groups in the encouragement of the formation of local or regional structures.

3) To itself initiate a limited programme or project.

4) To plan subsequent national conferences, which presumably would follow regional conferences.

5) To consider a public relations programme.

6) To consider the problems of financing labour education on a national level.

The resolution carried unanimously and those subsequently named to the committee were: Napoleon LeBlanc, Laval University; Father M.J. MacKinnon, St. Francis Xavier; Paul Guttman, University of Toronto; Stuart Jamieson and Dr. John Friesen, University of British Columbia; Gower Markle, United Steelworkers; Bert Hepworth, CBRE; Bill MacDonald, UAW; Fernand Jolicoeur, CCCL; Gordon Hawkins, CAAE; and myself representing the CLC.

While the conference was a Canadian affair, we were anxious to know more about what was happening in the United States and we invited two distinguished American educators, Joseph Mire, Executive Secretary of the Inter-University Labour Education Committee, and Eleanor Coit, Director of the American Labour Education Service. Mire told us that some 80 universities in the United States were rendering some form of service to labour groups, and he outlined some of the programmes. He was obviously impressed with our conference, describing it as "an historic event and a milestone in the development of labour education in Canada."

Coit, giving her impressions of the conference, said it reflected trends in labour education in many parts of the world. There was growing concern with the wider aspects of labour education as well as efforts to conduct education on all levels of leadership, use of the mass media, and recognition of the need to use all available resources.

In the years immediately following the conference, it was evident that the reunited labour movement, increased resources for labour education, and a sharper focus of objectives created a situation in which advantage should be taken of the growing interest in the university community. There was a new vitality and climate for labour education to develop.

But, in Canada, labour's interest and concern with education has never been restricted to areas directly related to union affairs. When the TLC first adopted a "Platform of Principles" at its 1898 convention at Winnipeg, the very first item on the list of objectives was "free compulsory education." That concern has continued through the years, and was clearly demonstrated in labour's participation in the Canadian Conferences on Education, held in 1958 and 1962. No single educational gathering in Canada had, or has since, brought together more high-level educators and such broad participation by other groups, nor attracted such public attention.

The chairman of the first conference, Dr. Wilder G. Penfield of Montreal, a world-renowned neurosurgeon, opening the first plenary session at Ottawa in February 1958, described it as "a spontaneous gathering without precedent." It was sponsored by 90 organizations, with a common interest in education, but otherwise remarkably dissimilar. In his address Dr. Penfield described education as the process of handing from one generation to another accumulated knowledge of the past and skills of the present, which, with courage, formed the fabric of Canada's defence and her best hopes for the future.

The gathering was composed of 850 delegates, representing Canadian organizations with a combined membership of about 3,000,000. They had assembled to examine the state of education in their country. The idea for the conference had originated in the Canadian Teachers' Federation, and was first suggested by Miss Caroline Robbins, a past-president. George Croskery, then Secretary of the Federation, became the actual architect of the conferences. In fall 1956 the Federation called a meeting of 26 national organizations to consider the possibilities of such a gathering. I represented the CLC and offered the support of the Congress.

The Soviet launching of the first sputnik in 1956 had sparked new interest in education. There was a feeling, stronger in the United States than in Canada, that this development indicated that the West was lagging behind the Soviet Union in science and technology. A few years later President John Kennedy vowed that the United States would be the first to land a man on the moon.

Among the dramatic measures taken by the Americans in their efforts to achieve superiority over the Soviets, was a reexamination of their educational system, with a view to bringing about fundamental changes, such as greater emphasis on basic education, science, and technology. It was not long before these precepts seeped into Canada, and so we became concerned about problems and inadequacies in the Canadian education system.

It was against this background that the first conference was held. Kurt Swinton, President of Encyclopedia Britannica (Canada), was chairperson, and I chaired the steering committee. Croskery was appointed Conference Director and Caroline Robbins had charge of office operations. The choice of a chairperson for plenary sessions presented some difficulty, particularly because of the political climate in Quebec, and Premier Duplessis' coolness to anything "national," extending even to the Governor General. However, when Dr. Penfield was suggested, he was unanimously and enthusiastically endorsed.

He proved to be considerably more than a tame honourary chairperson, making it apparent that he had definite ideas and deep convictions about education. There was some nervousness about what he might say, but his opening address was magnificent, simple yet profound, genuine, and sincere.

A characteristic Penfield occurrence took place during the Conference. Shortly after the first plenary session he told some of us that he was leaving for a few days, but, if possible, he would return before the conference ended. On the last day he telephoned me to say he was back, and he invited me, with my wife, to join him with some other Conference officers for cocktails before the closing banquet. As some of us gathered around him, bringing him up to date on what had transpired, he mentioned quite casually that he had just returned from Moscow.

"Moscow?" we asked in some amazement.

"Yes," he continued, explaining that a prominent Soviet scientist had received a serious brain injury in a car accident and the Soviet government had asked Dr. Penfield to go to Moscow for consultations. When he arrived he found that everything possible had already been done for the patient "And so, without unpacking my bags, I decided to return," he said.

To have known and worked with Dr. Penfield was, indeed, a great privilege.

While the first conference in 1959 had the full support of the participating organizations, there was considerable difference of opinion as to whether a second conference should be held. Some, including Croskery, thought that a follow-up conference would not generate the same interest and might be anticlimatic. There were also some, particularly within the Canadian Teachers' Federation, who were not enthusiastic about "non-professionals" becoming too involved in educational affairs, which they regarded as primarily their territory.

I did not share these views. I thought there was a need for more than one conference if meaningful improvements were to be made. This opinion was shared by a a majority of members of the Conference Committee. Before the first conference concluded, a resolution was passed in support of a second conference. There was explicit provision, however, that efforts to this end "should not duplicate the work of existing educational organizations."

It was planned to hold the second conference in the Royal York Hotel in Toronto three years later. But, as the date approached, the hotel became involved in a serious labour dispute with its employees, and there was no agreement in sight. The situation became of increasing concern, and there was considerable discussion, though I do not recall anyone favouring the conference being held in a strike-bound hotel. It was suggested that the conference might be postponed, or moved to another Toronto hotel.

I suggested the development might prove to be a blessing in disguise. The first conference had been held in Ontario, and it seemed to me to make good sense to hold the second conference in Montreal, particularly as Quebec had become involved. I pointed out that if the conference were held in a strike-bound hotel, not only would the labour representatives not attend, but they would probably withdraw from the organization. I realized that this sounded like an ultimatum, but I wanted the committee to understand labour's position. Kurt Swinton said that if there were a picket line, he would expect to see me on it and he would refuse to cross.

The arrangement with the Royal York was cancelled and the site was changed to the Queen Elizabeth Hotel in Montreal where the Second Canadian Conference on Education was held 4-8 March 1962. It attracted 2,013 delegates, and was described by Dr. J.F. Leddy, Vice-President of the University of Saskatchewan, as being "of unique character, without parallel in Canadian history, or, as far as I am aware, in the experience of other countries."

In the period between the two conferences there had been serious difficulties. In late 1959 and the early 1960s the affairs of the Conference were at a low ebb. It was one of the few times I had ever seen Kurt Swinton discouraged. I had stated publicly that we were broke and unless we received substantial financial assistance we would have to reconsider plans for the second conference. Swinton discussed the possibility of resigning. I tried to discourage him, and eventually he decided to carry on, actually becoming even more active.

He suggested we approach the Ford Foundation in New York for assistance. He knew some of the Foundation's officials and thought they might approve a request for a substantial grant for the Conference. At his invitation I went with him and we eventually received a grant of $100,000.

Prior to the second conference, eight areas were selected for pre-conference study:

1. The aims of education;
2. The professional status of teachers;
3. The development of student potential;
4. New dimensions of society;
5. Financing education;
6. Continuing education;
7. Research in education;
8. The citizen in education.

More than 150 contributors and correspondents were involved in the preparation of these studies, which were published in both French and English and distributed widely across the country.

The decision to move the conference from Toronto to Montreal meant a great deal of rearrangement, and the burden for much of this fell on Pauline McGibbon of Toronto. She was a highly efficient person who moved quickly and gracefully arranging one thing and changing another. No sudden revision seemed to ruffle her. We little knew that a few years later she would become Ontario's first woman Lieutenant-Governor.

A high priority of the Conference was to reach as many people as possible to stimulate their interest and involvement in education. To this end a group of 47 top public relations professionals was assembled to form a Public Relations Committee, headed by Kim McIlroy, Kurt Swinton's assistant. In addition, 30 Public Information Committees were formed in various centres and an extensive pre-conference programme was initiated, involving writing awards, a seminar for writers on education, and other forms of promotion. When the conference opened in Montreal there were 153 registered media correspondents.

The conference was designed as a three-tiered structure. The opening plenary session examined the question: "What does our society hope to achieve through education?" Following this, more than 2,000 delegates met in seven concurrent forums, each of which later divided into small work groups. Their findings and recommendations were reported to the closing plenary session.

Some weeks before the second conference opened I had considered resigning my conference office for a number of reasons, including increasing responsibilities within the Congress. I was to preside at the final plenary session, and then, with Swinton, close the conference. Before the session began I told him that I intended announcing my resignation. He did not respond as quickly as he usually did. He thought for a time, and then said: "Perhaps it is time we both resigned." And that is what happened.

It had become apparent that the Canadian Conference on Education was, in fact, folding up. As a result, the last few minutes of the closing session were most sombre. When the chairman's gavel finally came down there were tears in some eyes, and a great deal of embracing, kissing, and shaking of hands as we said goodbye to each other.

Both conferences were regarded as highly successful, but how do you actually measure the success of a conference? Surely not just by the publicity it receives or the excellence of its organization. I believe the real success must be measured by the degree to which its resolutions and recommendations are implemented.

Today, some 22 years later, a number of questions come to mind. Has education in Canada improved significantly since 1962? What impact did the Canadian Conferences on Education have on our educational systems? Were the problems in education, which were so expertly researched and eloquently discussed, resolved, even to a limited extent? How many of the resolutions and recommendations, which were prepared by thoughtful and dedicated men and women accepted by the delegates, have been implemented? Are our schools and universities of today better places for our children to acquire relevant skills, develop desirable human values, and learn critical thinking? Do our schools graduate students who are more aware of the world in which they live and more concerned about the lives of people everywhere? Do they have the knowledge, the strength, and the wisdom to mould for themselves, and for others, more meaningful lives? And were the thought-provoking statements of the speakers at these conferences just the expression of pious generalities, to be heard once, agreed upon, and then forgotten?

Today, what one speaker described as "the suffocating burden of armaments" has not been reduced; it has increased. Universities are increasingly facing difficult financial problems, and so the preoccupation of university presidents and others is in the main budgetary. The needs of higher education are too-often determined by the demands of the fiscal year. Few academic reasons are given for decisions which affect many services, facilities, and programmes. Surely a university is not a business, education is not a product, and the student is not just the consumer of the product.

As I see education in Canada today, I can point to very little improvement since 1962, except in the field of adult continuing education. The problem is not only that of money. I do not agree with the view of Dr. A.W. Trueman, who at the 1958 conference said: "Nothing is wrong with the Canadian education that a great deal of money will not put straight." This implies more of the same, and that is not good enough.

We need more money, to be sure, but we also need the kind of education that is more creative, more thought-provoking, experimental, and relevant to the kind of world we are living in. In this regard we have made very little progress since 1962. Is now the right time for another Conference on Education?

CHAPTER TEN
The Labour College of Canada

IT IS NATURAL THAT LABOUR'S main educational interest should be directed to meeting specific trade union needs. The idea of a permanent labour educational centre, with a fairly advanced curriculum, had long been a dream of the labour movement in Canada. It became a reality in 1963 when the Labour College of Canada was established as an independent institution, through the co-operation of the University of Montreal, McGill University, and the CLC. It had long been recognized that there was increasing need within the movement for sustained basic studies in the humanities and social sciences, as well as advanced specialized instruction in the theory and practice of trade unionism. For as social, economic, and political problems arise, multiply, and become more complex, the need for the training and education of present and future union leaders increases proportionately.

Talk of establishing a Labour College dated all the way back to 1886. In that year Brian Lynch, a Knights of Labor delegate from Toronto, sponsored a motion to introduce an educational programme in the union movement in Canada. At the 1911 convention of the TLC, a motion was adopted calling for the establishment of a Labour College. Then, almost half a century later, the convention of the CLC held in Winnipeg in 1958 gave unanimous support to a resolution instructing the Congress officers to "explore the possibility of establishing a Labour College, in co-operation with an appropriate university." The long-cherished dream might at long last be realized.

As the Congress Director of Education when the resolution was passed, I knew I would have the privilege and honour of being closely involved in the realization of such a college, and, indeed, be one of its founders. I was very excited about being connected with such an innovative project, reflecting many of my personal ideals and aspirations. The fact that so many people before had seen the importance and value of a Labour College reinforced my own conviction of its necessity. It had the blessing of our predecessors and now the consent of our contemporaries.

In the excitement and enthusiasm of those first affirmative actions I did not, and indeed could not, anticipate the endless negotiations, the reticence of many of the people involved, the skepticism of others, and the frustrations. I did not foresee the five long years of meetings and negotiations, persuading, wrangling, sometimes compromising, and always impatiently waiting for all the jigsaw pieces of this complex undertaking to fall in place. Many times during those five years I felt discouraged and unhappy about the slow and tedious progress. It was difficult for me to understand why an idea that seemed to me to have so many advantages would not be immediately and unconditionally accepted. Nevertheless, notwithstanding the dejection and the stumbling blocks, I deeply believed that one day, in my lifetime, the Labour College of Canada would become a reality.

The idea of such a college had been rekindled and began to germinate in my mind about a year after the merger. Gradually its shape and form began to mould, and I tried to assess the possibilities of success and the consequences of failure. I wondered when, and with whom, I should discuss it. Finally I decided to raise the matter first at a meeting of the CLC Education Advisory Committee in fall 1957, just prior to the CLC's Winnipeg convention.

The committee members, all labour educators in their respective unions, reacted most enthusiastically. They included: Gower Markle, United Steelworkers; John Whitehouse, Textile Workers' Union of America; Bert Hepworth, CBRE; and Alan Schroeder, UAW. They, with others, shared my views about the need and timeliness of such a college. John Whitehouse, who was a graduate of Ruskin College, an institute of this type in England, spoke with particular eloquence and characteristic enthusiasm in support. There was no question in the minds of the committee members about labour support, and some proposed concrete steps that the CLC Education Department should take in pursuit of the project.

I told the committee that, before discussing the subject with the Congress officers, I wanted to have their reaction and recommendations. The committee then decided unanimously to ask the officers and the Congress Executive Council: "To give serious and favourable consideration to the establishment of a Labour College, if possible in co-operation with an appropriate university."

Shortly after that meeting I discussed the recommendation with Stanley Knowles, who was at that time an Executive Vice-President of the congress. His first reaction was encouraging but cautious. Knowing Stanley well, I did not expect an electrifying outburst of enthusiasm. He pondered for a while and finally said he liked the idea and supported it in principle. Slowly, he began to ask a number of specific and cogent questions. He wanted to know how the college would be structured, who would be eligible to attend, where it would be located, how much it would cost to operate, where the funds would come from and, finally, what would be the responsibility of the Canadian Labour Congress. At that point I could give only cautious answers.

My next move was to approach the other Congress officers. I recall that my first discussion with them was rather frustrating. As I entered the boardroom I sensed that they seemed to be preoccupied with other urgent matters. They certainly did not show the same enthusiasm as had members of the Educational Advisory Committee, yet I could not expect that. I remember well President Jodoin's opening remark as I sat down: "Well Max, what are you getting us into now?" But there was no hostility in his voice; he asked the question in his usual kind and friendly manner.

As I outlined my concept of the college, I was unable to judge what impression I was making. I had the feeling that I was not being very convincing. President Jodoin was looking at me with a noncommittal expression. Secretary-Treasurer Donald MacDonald did not look at me at all. He continued writing and seemed detached from the proceedings. Executive Vice-President Bill Dodge sat reclined in his chair, watching me with expressionless eyes. Only in Stanley Knowles' expression did I see support and encouragement. Even before I concluded my presentation, I felt that the timing of the meeting was not right, and that I could not expect the much-needed support.

Following my presentation, President Jodoin said that the idea was very interesting and, if the Congress were to promote it and become fully involved, it would mean a considerable commitment. Consequently, before supporting the idea, even in principle, the officers would have to give the matter a great deal of serious consideration. He concluded by saying that, in due course, I would be asked to meet with them again for a more detailed discussion. On this optimistic note I was about to leave, when he called me back. "Max," he said, "You stated your case very well." I thanked him and left. I knew he sensed my disappointment.

Some weeks later I learned from Stanley Knowles that the officers did indeed support the idea of a Labour College, but they had serious doubts about the support the college would receive from the labour movement. It was this uncertainty that was the key factor in their reluctance officially to endorse the college, thus allowing me to campaign for its establishment.

Months later, when the Congress convention was held in Winnipeg, in June 1958, the Congress officers still had not made a decision. I then decided on another approach, which I discussed with Gower Markle, who was also at the convention. We prepared a resolution calling on the officers to explore the possibility of establishing a college. We then conspired with one of the delegates, Jimmy Graham of the Carpenters' Union, to sponsor the resolution by submitting it to the resolutions committee. That body moved concurrence and the resolution was adopted by the convention unanimously.

I was thrilled and excited. Markle and I realized that, for the first time, we, the present generation of labour educators, had positive and unequivocal support for a Labour College, because the "Parliament of Labour," as Congress conventions were sometimes described, had so decided. That was it!

In the following months I drafted a memorandum for my own guidance, setting out various aspects of the undertaking, including the structure, the budget, the curriculum, and other matters. Having no previous experience with such an institution, I wanted all aspects to evolve from discussions. I relied on the Education Advisory Committee, as well as others, for guidance and assistance in the preparation of a concrete and comprehensive outline of the project.

Once the CLC approved my memorandum in principle in 1959, I began what proved to be a long and often frustrating trek to universities. Beginning with President Davidson Dunton of Carleton University in Ottawa, I reviewed the background of the CLC's decision to promote a Labour College. I gave an overview of the educational programmes conducted within the labour movement and explained the need for a permanent institution for advanced education and training. I then invited Carleton University to become associated with the college.

Dr. Dunton expressed interest and asked what was expected from the university in terms of financial obligations, facilities, and participation. I explained that we did not expect the university to contribute money, but we would like the university to nominate a number of people to serve on the Board of Governors, which would be responsible for the entire operation of the college. We also expected the university to play a leading role in designing and guiding the academic programme. Finally, we expected the university to supply the necessary physical plant.

Dr. Dunton said he regarded our request as very important, but he worried about possible complications. He said he would consider the matter carefully and would discuss it with his colleagues. I felt our first meeting concluded on a friendly and hopeful note.

Not having heard from him after several months, I arranged a second meeting. At that time Dr. Dunton was particularly interested in knowing just what the responsibility of the CLC would be, and to what extent it would be involved in college affairs. He gave the impression of being concerned that the Congress would dominate the whole operation. I explained that the Labour College was intended to be an independent educational institution. The CLC, like the university, would designate representatives to the Board of Governors. The CLC would undertake to raise the necessary funds. Moreover, if the university wanted equal representation on the Board, or even more, I saw no difficulty with such an arrangement.

He seemed satisfied with my explanation and suggested I meet with Dean James A. Gibson of the Faculty of Arts and Science for a more-detailed discussion. Two or three months later we finally met, then we met again, and again. In November 1959 we managed to agree on a joint memorandum to be submitted to the Carleton University and the Congress. It stated in part:

Carleton University undertakes to teach certain agreed-upon courses. It shall assign instructors for and determine the contents of such courses. The balance of the programme shall be taught by the Labour College. It shall determine the content of such courses and recruit teaching personnel. The Labour College will also be fully responsible for the administration, recruiting of students, fund raising, etc., for the College. The full scheduled programme shall be conducted on the University Campus. However, activities not regularly scheduled may be held outside the University Campus.

In other words, the programme was to be divided, with the University and the College teaching their respective agreed-upon parts of the programme, and the College responsible for all College affairs. This was not the best kind of arrangement. Nevertheless, I reluctantly agreed in order to get the College off the ground. When I presented the memorandum to the Congress officers they did not seem very happy about it. I then suggested that I try to arrange a meeting of a high-level committee of Carleton with the Congress officers.

Early in February 1960 such a meeting took place. Carleton was represented by Dr. Dunton, Dr. Gibson, Professor John Porter, and Professor Gordon Scott. The CLC was represented by Donald MacDonald, Stanley Knowles, Norman Dowd, and myself. After about an hour and a half of inconclusive discussion, Dr. Dunton said he would send us a letter in which he would state specifically the university's position concerning possible involvement. On 16 February 1960, I received a letter from Dr. Gibson which read in part:

I think I ought to report to you that within the University Committee which has been following the proposed Labour College question there are still strong views on two particular points:

1) We are concerned with what the October 5, 1959, memorandum described as a *divided* programme. In the minds of my colleagues this is *not* a *joint* programme, and they are, therefore, understandably concerned with what the form or direction of a divided programme may eventually be; and, in particular, the responsibility of the Director proposed to be appointed from the CLC side.

2) The simplest administrative provision for a *divided* programme would be the physical separation of the two parts of the programme (as the October 5, 1959, memorandum suggests), preferably separation in time. Though this is the simplest provision, it may not be the best; all I would like you to know is that some among my colleagues are insistent upon this separation, and I feel there will have to be some meeting of minds upon this point before we can resolve some other questions which hinge upon it.

Needless to say, we were somewhat shocked by Carleton's insistence on a "physical separation" of the programme. Donald MacDonald, like all of us, was outraged at the idea that Labour College students could attend sessions for which Carleton would be responsible on the university campus, but, sessions on trade unionism, for which the College would assume responsibility, would have to be given off campus.

After more than a year of discussions with Carleton University, during which my hopes sometimes rose and sometimes fell, this last Carleton letter was a deep disappointment. We did not meet again.

In retrospect, I had the impression that in some respects Carleton wanted to co-operate with the CLC, but, as this was the first time that the labour movement in Canada had approached a university jointly to sponsor a labour college, the university was seriously concerned about possible repercussions from its corporate contributors.

After the termination of discussions with Carleton University the Education Advisory Committee recommended that I approach the University of Western Ontario in London. I was not as enthusiastic about a possible association with Western as were some of the other committee members, but, as the university was located in a highly unionized area, I went along with the recommendation.

When I met with President James Hall of Western, I outlined our ideas concerning the college, including its purpose, programme, structure, finances, and other matters. I emphasized that we neither expected nor wanted the college to be an integral part of the university structure, nor even to have an association similar to that existing between Ruskin College and Oxford University in England. I explained what we believed to be a suitable association and invited Western's participation in the joint project.

Dr. Hall said a Labour College in Canada was an excellent idea and should certainly be encouraged. He had some reservations, however, about its practicality, and indeed the usefulness of a university-labour joint project. He believed it would be more advantageous to the labour movement if the college were administered by the CLC alone. Nevertheless, he said he would discuss the matter with other university officials. His personal view, however, was that for the time being the University of Western Ontario should not become involved. While he did not attempt to justify or explain his opinion, it was quite clear and forthright. I accepted his view in the same spirit that it was expressed.

When we decided to approach Western we had obviously overlooked the fact that the Labour College was to be a bilingual institution. Had we made arrangements with Western it would have been difficult, if not impossible, to conduct the programme effectively in both French and English. For our purpose that was not the right university, and perhaps this too was one of the reasons for Dr. Hall's reticence.

During the many months of discussions with the universities, my department was preoccupied with a wide range of activities, and so, after my experience with the University of Western Ontario, the matter of the Labour College was again shelved, much to my chagrin. I was becoming quite discouraged with the reluctance of university officials. In the fall of 1960, however, I resumed my efforts to find a university that would be willing to co-operate with us. I arranged to meet Professor H.D. Woods, the Dean of Industrial Relations at McGill University in Montreal. He had been recognized for a number of years as an authority in the field of industrial relations and was trusted by most people in the labour movement, and well-regarded for his honesty, fairness, and objectivity. He listened to my explanation of our plans and hopes and of the discussions with Carleton and Western. He showed keen and concentrated interest and when I concluded I saw he was absorbed in thought. He was silent for a long time.

Then, leaning forward in his chair and looking directly at me, he said: "Max, the idea of a Labour College in Canada is fascinating. I would like to see McGill associated with such a college. I am more than willing to try to see this realized." He continued, explaining that McGill's association with the college would first have to be approved by the University's Board of Governors. He undertook to discuss the matter with Professor J.R. Mallory, Head of the Political Science Department, who, he thought, would co-operate.

Our first discussion ended on that note. I was elated, for this was the first encouraging and unequivocal expression of support that I had received from a university official in almost two years.

Several weeks later Professor Woods, Professor Mallory, who had agreed to work with us, and I met. Among other matters we discussed their recommendation that the University of Montreal be also invited to become a participant. They pointed out that the location of the college in Montreal, and the collaboration of both a French-speaking and an English-speaking university would make possible a completely bilingual and bicultural institution. I readily agreed, knowing the officers of the Congress would support such an idea. Professor Woods undertook to discuss the matter with Professor Gilles Beausoleil, Director of Industrial Relations at the University of Montreal.

Early in November 1960, I met with Professors Woods, Mallory, and Beausoleil. We realized that if the two universities were to consider becoming involved they would require an outline of what the Labour College was all about. We proceeded, somewhat laboriously, to draft such an outline. This included all the main aspects of the college — its purpose, structure, budget, staff, and other matters. It was a significant document, and constituted the first comprehensive outline drafted in concrete terms, thus setting the whole affair in focus. The outline served not only as a basis of discussion by the universities, the Congress, and others, but it was also used extensively in the fund-raising and recruiting campaigns in the two years preceding the opening of the college.

When the document was completed, we agreed that we would discuss it with our respective institutions and then try to arrange a meeting of the heads of the two universities with the officers of the Congress. I suggested to President Jodoin that he send invitations for such a meeting, and in due course it was held on 11 November 1960 at the Cercle Universitaire in Montreal. From McGill University came Principal Cyril James, James Mallory, Michael Oliver, and Edward Webster. From the University of Montreal: Monsignor René Lussier, Philippe Garigue, Maurice Bouchard, Jean Réal Cardin, and André Raynauld. From the CLC: Claude Jodoin, Donald MacDonald, Stanley Knowles, William Dodge, and myself.

I was delighted with the representation, but the meeting was by no means smooth sailing for those of us who were so anxious to get an agreement and have the college launched. The discussion was very friendly, informal, and at times even jovial; yet I felt the presence of some strain. Basically, the universities really wanted to co-operate, I was sure of that, but they were not sure about the advisability and practicality of establishing an autonomous Labour College at that time. They were concerned, among other things, about the estimated high cost of running the college and they questioned the degree of support that would come from the trade union movement. Nevertheless, I believe that meeting contributed, perhaps more than any other, to the eventual launching and development of the college. The various views of the participants contributed significantly to the eventual establishment of the Labour College of Canada.

Claude Jodoin presided. He stated that the object of the meeting was to study and discuss the possible creation of a Labour College, following the work of the committee formed the previous year, representing the three institutions. He asked Professor Mallory to report for the committee.

After giving a detailed report on the background, Mallory summed up the committee's views as follows:

The committee felt that it is essential that the Labour College be constituted as an autonomous entity, largely independent of the institutions founding it. The universities would assume responsibility in academic matters and in supplying staff; the CLC, for its part, would be responsible for assuring enrollment and securing finances. The College would be administered by the Board of Governors, composed of three representatives named by McGill University, three by the University of Montreal, and four by the CLC. The founding institutions would thus retain a certain control, but only indirectly through the right to appoint to the Board. The Board, on the other hand, would be responsible for the policy and administration of the College. The Board would name a permanent administrative officer with whom would co-operate, according to university traditions, the academic senate made up of the faculty.

In conclusion, he pointed out that the Labour College which was envisaged could be seen as a unique, original, and truly national institution. He then suggested that a continuing committee was necessary to speed the establishment of the college.

Dr. James said he was struck by the high cost of the project. He felt he should state explicitly that McGill could not contribute financially. He wanted to know from Claude Jodoin whether he was confident about raising the necessary funds. Given the high cost, Dr. James said it seemed to him that other similar but less costly methods for achieving the objective should be examined. He wondered whether it would not be possible to use existing facilities in the universities, and to have special courses prepared to meet the CLC's needs. Such a procedure, he said, would obviously cost less.

President Jodoin replied that he saw this meeting only as a first step in the realization of our goals. We wished to know first if the universities were willing to collaborate with us in an educational exercise for the benefit of our members. We did not feel that it was possible at this time to fix the final form which these activities might take. Personally, I was not very happy with his reply, as I saw no need to question the willingness of the universities to collaborate. I felt that the discussions we had had with them for almost a year, and the report of the University-CLC Committee, were ample confirmation of that. However, I said nothing at that stage.

Monsignor Lussier said that the University of Montreal was ready to collaborate in the work of developing and training leadership, there should be no doubt from the outset of the university's intentions. An excerpt from the minutes reads:

He stated that he, nevertheless, shared some of the concerns of Dr. James. He had asked the representatives of the University of Montreal on the Labour College Committee if the existing facilities of the university, and especially the present organization of extension work, could not fill the needs of the CLC adequately. If this were the case, he continued, the two main obstacles which he could see in the way of founding a Labour College would be avoided: (a) the high cost of the enterprise, and (b) the dispersion of the efforts of the university professors involved.

The minutes continued:

Dr. James said that he would add to what Monsignor Lussier had just stated that there were additional difficulties raised by the prospect of courses during the daytime, throughout the academic year, which would involve the presence on the campus, and in the lecture halls of students who did not have the same academic standing as regular students.

This observation by Dr. James was dumbfounding. Once again it was intimated that a trade unionist would just not fit into a university environment. Carleton University had expressed a similar view. However, I did not realize that other university people shared Dr. James' opinion. No one commented on it, but I spoke up, feeling the discussion was developing outside the main issues. I underlined clearly that it was impossible to create a truly-national, permanent institution, such as we desired, without agreeing to the Labour College formula. On the other hand, we had to know the exact details of the project before it could be placed before our membership. This was why we could not, at that time, estimate precisely the support we would receive from our members.

Dr. James observed that he had already mentioned that the Labour College could be seen as taking a number of forms. Monsignor Lussier added that a number of approaches could be studied, but basically the question was one of finance. Other participants expressed their views, most of which were peripheral to the basic issue, seeking an acceptable alternative. Finally Donald MacDonald brought the discussion into focus. The minutes recorded:

> Mr. MacDonald expressed the deep interest of the CLC in the Labour College. There was no question of whether or not the College would come into being. It would undoubtedly be founded some day, if not now then later. What required immediate attention, therefore, was the question of whether or not the present was the appropriate time for a decision, and if current conditions were favourable to its founding. The CLC was quite convinced that the College should be set up. But its attitude was that it was best to walk before attempting to run. Was the scheme presented to the meeting the best one? He did not know. But one thing, he felt, was certain. The CLC could not found the College on its own; it needed the co-operation of the universities in one way or another. The CLC was ready to assume financial responsibility for the College; it would pay whatever it would cost. But, in spite of his great respect for Principal James, and his long experience, Mr. MacDonald could not see how the Principal's conception of the College could be realized unless the objective of a permanent national institution was accepted. Once the CLC was assured of the collaboration of the universities, it could go to its members and try to get their support. The purpose of the present meeting, as he saw it, was to agree, if possible, on the principles of, first, university co-operation in the Labour College project; and, second on the appropriateness of continuing to work toward this through a committee.

Donald MacDonald expressed his views in a clear, precise, and most agreeable fashion. As he spoke I could feel the impact he was making on others and I was delighted with his contribution. Professor Oliver agreed with MacDonald's understanding of the objective of the meeting. It seemed necessary, he said, to know whether the proposed structure of the Labour College was acceptable. Dr. James said MacDonald was asking the meeting to choose the most difficult path. An autonomous college raised a number of difficulties in regard to the existing regulations of the universities. At McGill, he said, only the Board of Governors had the power to admit students, to appoint faculty, and to approve curriculum.

Monsignor Lussier said his university's support for the proposed college, in whatever form, was assured. Finally, Claude Jodoin referred to the terms of reference of the University-CLC Committee, and suggested the committee be empowered to explore and study all the different proposals which had been made at the meeting. His suggestion was accepted and the meeting adjourned.

A few days later I was asked to meet with the officers. We reviewed some of the reservations expressed by Principal James and Rector Lussier. Jodoin asked whether we should, in fact, rule out a more modest project, perhaps some compromise between the Labour College formula and some of the alternatives suggested by the universities.

I shook my head emphatically, saying: "No, no, no." I pointed out that the memorandum on the college, which had been submitted to the Congress and the universities, was the product of a lengthy analysis and discussion with the representatives of the universities. The fact that the university principals had asked that consideration be given to alternatives did not necessarily mean that they rejected the original formula.

"Moreover, Mr. President," I went on, "your mandate from the 1958 convention calls for the establishment of an identifiable Labour College and not some kind of University-CLC joint educational scheme."

"But," interjected Donald MacDonald, "your own estimated cost of running the College is very high; where will the money come from? You say it will come from our unions, and perhaps some provincial governments. Well, I have strong reservations about this."

"I'm afraid I don't share your views," I replied, somewhat impatiently, "but that is not important. What is important is that we make the approach to our unions. Mr. President, we will never know what response we will get from our affiliates until we approach them. We will never know. Let me try."

I am sure it was obvious to the officers that I did not favour a compromise formula. I was adamant in the pursuit of this long-cherished dream and I felt very deeply about it. They could have overruled my obstinate position, but they did not. They could have instructed met to negotiate a more modest arrangement, but they did not. I think they sensed my commitment, and for the first time I knew I had their full support.

The joint committee then met several times. We examined the alternative proposals which had been made by Principal James and Rector Lussier, but we decided to stay with the original formula, although we did make some technical changes. The final draft was then submitted to the two universities and the Congress for approval.

It was not until June 1961 that the universities made the positions known. When the University-CLC Committee met, Professor Mallory reported that the project had been considered by both the Senate and the Board of Governors at McGill. He had personally presented the project to the Senate, which welcomed and approved it. The Board of Governors had also approved the scheme, but with a few additional technical conditions which were accepted without difficulty.

Professor Raynauld reported for the University of Montreal. He said that, in the course of any discussions on the proposal, a new element had emerged, namely the absence of the Confederation of National Trade Unions (CNTU). This was the Quebec-based central body of what had originally been a "confessional" type organization, then known as the Canadian and Catholic Confederation of Labour (CCCL). Although he was instructed to report that the university approved the college project, it asked (I could only assume as a condition of support) that the CNTU be invited to participate. He said Dean Garigue had been instructed to meet with CNTU representatives to ascertain their interest. When he met Jean Marchand,

President of the CNTU, and Fernand Jolicoeur, the Director of Education, Marchand had greeted him with: "I have been expecting you for the past two years." Dean Garigue said Marchand expressed some concern that the CNTU had not been invited to participate earlier. Raynauld concluded that it was possible the University of Montreal would not approve the scheme if in doing so it risked public criticism from Marchand and the CNTU.

This was, indeed, a new element. We had never considered inviting the CNTU to join the project, nor were we aware of their interest. I had no objection to their participation, but I had no idea what the reaction of the Congress officers would be. Nevertheless, I agreed with the committee's recommendation that the CNTU be invited to meet with the committee on the following day if possible.

The next day Oliver and I met with Jean Marchand and Fernand Jolicoeur. Marchand expressed surprise that the proposal had been drafted without any consultation with the CNTU. He said it had first been called to his attention by a visit from Dean Garigue. Because they had not been involved earlier, it was impossible for him to express an official point of view, which would commit his executive committee. However, he was willing to proceed as if the CNTU's approval had been given, and he asked Jolicoeur to take part in the meetings of our committee, as though he were an official delegate. I was satisfied with his conditional support.

When I reported to the Congress officers, I was pleasantly surprised that they agreed to the CNTU's participation without question. With that problem solved, both universities endorsed the original concept of the Labour College. In the months that followed the Joint Committee expanded and refined the original memorandum. We then asked the universities and the Congress to nominate their representatives to the Board of Governors, which we proposed should meet for the first time 31 January 1961.

The Board was composed of 19 members — five from McGill University, five from the University of Montreal, six from the CLC, and three from the CNTU. It was a very prestigious group consisting of three industrialists, a judge, six professors, and nine trade unionists. At the first meeting officers were chosen unanimously: R.E. Powell, Chairman; Justice André Montpetit, Co-chairman and Chairman of the Executive Committee; Stanley Knowles, Vice-Chairman; Max Swerdlow, Registrar; Fernand Jolicoeur, Recording Secretary.

Other members of the fist Board were: H.D. Woods, J.R. Mallory, T.R. McLagan, and J.G. Notman from McGill; A. Morel, A. Raynauld, G. Rocher, and G. Beausoleil from the University of Montreal; J. Morris, G. Burt, G. Markle, W.J. Smith, and Roger Provost from the CLC; J. Marchand and R. Martel from the CNTU.

The fact that R.E. Powell undertook to be chairman was both interesting and remarkable. He was the Chancellor of McGill, but better known as an extremely prominent industrialist and a pioneer in the aluminum industry, both in Canada and throughout the world. He was the chief architect and driving force behind the Aluminum Company of Canada (ALCAN) projects at Arvida, Quebec, and Kitimat, B.C., the two largest aluminum smelters in the world. What was even more remarkable was that the trade unionists on the board, all of whom were national leaders, supported Powell's nomination.

He was a good chairman. Although 76 years of age, he seldom, if ever, missed a meeting or an important college function. In those formative years, when many difficult problems came before the Board, his judgment and guidance was always well-balanced and objective. He presided over meetings in a reasoned, dignified and efficient manner. It soon became apparent to all of us that he very sincerely wanted the college to succeed. I recall when, after the first meeting of the Board of Governors, I walked with him to his car, he said: "I believe this college is not only good for your trade unions, it is also good for my university."

In my capacity as registrar I saw him frequently and I never had any difficulty in doing so. Once, when I was in his well-appointed office discussing some college problems, he leaned back in his chair and stared at me with his gray, searching eyes. Then, as if he had not heard a word I said, he smiled and commented: "Max, you must have been quite a radical in your youth." "No sir," I quickly replied, "I was not just a radical, I was a communist." We both laughed; I think he appreciated the remark.

On another occasion, when we were looking for a full-time principal for the College, someone recommended a person at Ruskin College in England, who wanted to come to Canada. None of us knew the man. Powell said he would make some enquiries and several weeks later he called me to his office and told me that he had some information about the prospective principal, explaining: "I think he is somewhat to the left of Wilson (the Labour Prime Minister), but he is a good man. If he is interested in the post it is all right with me." For various reasons the man did not come.

In our fund-raising campaigns I never approached ALCAN for a contribution, nor did we receive one unsolicited. I did approach Powell once with regard to financing. This was at a time when we desperately needed operating funds. After a meeting of the Board of Governors, just before the members left, I went to Powell and quietly told him of my financial problem. I said I needed $3,000 as soon as possible, and asked if he had any suggestions.

He was silent for a moment, and then said: "I think I have a suggestion; let me try." He called over Notman and McLagan, the two other industrialists on the Board, and he said: "Look here, Max needs $3,000 right now. I am giving him $1,000. Will you each give him $1,000?" They agreed and that was all there was to it. It was really not a question he asked his fellow governors; it sounded more like a challenge. Several days later I received the money.

R.E. Powell was chairman of the Board of Governors for seven years, and then, because of failing health, he relinquished the position at the age of 83. He died in 1973 in his 86th year.

A portion of his obituary read:

As the first chairman of the (Labour) College in 1962 he worked with Max Swerdlow of the Canadian Labour Congress, Dean H.D. Woods of McGill, Judge André Montpetit, Hon. Jean Marchand then of the CNTU, and J.G. Notman to establish this institution of higher learning for trade union members.

Mr. Powell served as chairman of the Labour College for seven years, fervent in this belief that labour-management relations could be improved through broader educational opportunities, not only for management staffs, but also for union leaders.

I am more than glad to have known and worked with the first chairman of the Labour College of Canada, R.E. Powell.

At the first meeting of the Board of Governors, we finalized a number of issues regarding the college structure, programme, and staff. What remained was the launching of a national campaign to raise our objective of $240,000 to cover the anticipated cost of operating the college and granting scholarships for the first three years. We referred to these years as the experimental period.

As registrar, it was my responsibility to raise the money. I was confident we would be supported because we had a good cause, and so I undertook the task happily. I planned the campaign with some precision. First, I listed the unions that already had educational programmes within their own institution. Experience led me to believe that such unions would be the first to support the college, both with grants and by financing their own participants. As our campaign progressed, this assessment proved correct.

Secondly, bearing in mind our objective of $240,000, I listed the specific amount I would request from each of the prospective contributors, or the very small unions. I knew the Steelworkers and Auto Workers would contribute generously, as they did. In the case of the small unions, I just did not know their financial resources, and so I gladly accepted whatever they contributed, which in some cases was as low as $10 or $25 for each of the first three years.

I also approached the federal and provincial governments for contributions of specific amounts. I met with the federal Minister of Labour Milton Gregg and received the amount I requested. I followed this up with meetings with almost all the provincial ministers of labour and education. In Ontario and Nova Scotia, I also met with the Premiers.

In those days there were some in the labour movement who were a bit critical of us for asking governments to make financial contributions to our educational activities. They believed that governments would not allocate funds unconditionally without some "strings." They also thought government donors might want to influence the direction of the college and the substance of the programme, maintaining that "he who pays the piper calls the tune."

I never held that view. I believed government funds were public funds and should be allocated to all types of education. It was, in fact, incumbent upon a government to allocate some funds to worker education.

There is some personal gratification in knowing that this position has now been universally accepted, at least in countries where free trade unions exist. Today there is no difference of opinion on whether or not to accept government money for worker education. In fact, in many cases, the view is that generally, governments are not giving enough to support such activities. In my experience, in soliciting funds for the College, governments have never placed any conditions or "strings," not even accountability, on the contribution. I did not approach any industries for contributions, but I did ask a few industries to provide scholarships to enable their employees to attend the college.

The financial campaign began with a circular letter signed by CLC President Claude Jodoin and Secretary-Treasurer Donald MacDonald. This was sent to all affiliated central bodies and unions, requesting support through the sponsorship of students and by financial contributions. I then undertook a tour across Canada, speaking to as many organizations as possible. It took about two months to visit the main centres, coast to coast.

Both unions and governments responded admirably. Most trade union publications, and in many cases the daily press, carried accounts of the college. The campaign succeeded beyond our expectations and we far exceeded our objective. The launching of the college was now assured.

Our original plan for the first eight-week term was to have two classes: one in the French language with a minimum of 15 students, and one in the English language with a maximum of 30 students. There were to be five fields of study: economics, history, political science, sociology, and trade unionism in theory and practice. We planned to grant ten scholarships of $1,000 each. When the college opened on 3 June 1963, there were 32 French language and 53 English language students, and the college disbursed $19,000 in scholarships.

The opening ceremony was an emotional and momentous occasion for those of us who had worked so hard toward the establishment of the college. As the programme progressed I thought of the many events and trials over the previous five years. Now all our hopes and some of our misgivings were crystalized in this historic event. I felt something new had been added to Canadian education in general, while expanding the horizons and creating a place specifically dedicated to labour education in Canada.

As we sat on the platform I was extremely happy, excited, and even triumphant. Surrounded by officers and students, here at last were the tangible results of our efforts. It was a very important moment, not only in my career and my personal life, and I could hardly prevent a lump rising in my throat when President Jodoin said in his address: "Max Swerdlow never doubted the possibility of establishing the Labour College. His perseverance, more than that of any other single individual, has brought this dream to reality."

When I got up to speak I had great difficulty containing my emotions. The opening ceremonies concluded with a gala reception and the Labour College of Canada formally came into being.

The administration was made up of eleven professors, a number of guest lecturers, the registrar, two office secretaries, two co-principals, and an assistant to the principals and a librarian. In addition, there was the Board of Governors, the Executive Committee, the Administrative Committee, and 26 Labour College representatives, most of whom were engaged at universities across the country, who interviewed and evaluated student applicants.

One of the difficulties in completing the college structure was finding a suitably qualified principal. We were fortunate that Dean Woods and Gilles Beausoleil agreed to be co-principals for the first term despite their heavy loads in their own universities. In the meantime we continued a search for someone to fill the post on a full-time basis.

At a meeting of the Board of Governors someone recommended we approach Pierre Trudeau of the University of Montreal as a person who might be interested. I contacted him and we arranged to meet for lunch in the Hunt Club at the Mount Royal Hotel. He knew, of course, that I wanted to speak to him about the Labour College, but he did not know that, on behalf of the Board of Governors, I would offer him the position of principal at an annual salary of $12,000.

As I proceeded to explain the programme and objectives of the college, the people who were on the Board of Governors, the support we were receiving, and other details, his expressive eyes were constantly fixed on me. He listened attentively, sometimes nodding his head in approval, other times gently smiling. Throughout my full explanation he did not interrupt once. I concluded with the invitation to become principal, mentioning, of course, the salary.

After that I had another gin and tonic and while we proceeded with our meal we talked about a variety of things, but not about my offer. I thought he might be interested, otherwise he would have said so right away, but I was wrong. He told me that he quite familiar with the college from newspaper accounts and from some of his colleagues and that he very much liked the whole concept. Then he was silent for a time. When he resumed, he said he very much appreciated the offer, and that under other circumstances he would certainly accept, but he could not at that time. He explained that Premier Duplessis had prevented him from teaching at the university for a number of years. At the time of our meeting, he had been back for only about a year and he wanted to continue his career at the university.

Naturally, I was sorry he did not accept our offer, but I was much impressed with his precise, lucid, yet warm explanation. He spoke softly, but with vibrance; his words seemed to roll out so eloquently and yet so simply. When he finished I was almost hypnotized and at a loss for words. I told him I fully understood the reason for his decision, and I did not pursue the matter further. Had Pierre Elliot Trudeau accepted our offer, the history of Canada would probably have been different.

Professors Woods and Beausoleil continued as part-time principals during the second term in 1964, and then we engaged Professor Fernand Martin of the University of Montreal as the first full-time principal in 1965. His academic background in economics, his deep interest in social problems, and his interest and enthusiasm for the college made him a unanimous choice.

Shortly after the first session an interesting development took place. Prior to the establishment of the college the Canadian Labour Congress had been asked by the Department of External Affairs to undertake a six month training programme for a few foreign trade unionists who would be fully financed by the Colombo Plan. The CLC agreed, and I was asked to take charge of the programme.

In the first year, two trade unionists came from India, and in the second year four came from Malaysia. Although the External Aid Office was willing to support a greater number, not many were able to take six months off their jobs to come and study in Canada. When the Labour College became operational, I approached the External Aid Officer with the recommendation that foreign trade union students be invited to attend the college for the regular session of two months, and then visit industrial centres for another month. The recommendation was accepted and we made the arrangements regarding finances, invitations, post-college programmes, and other matters.

The second session of the college, commencing in March 1964, was attended by 19 foreign trade unionists from the Caribbean, Asia, and Africa. Each subsequent year the number of foreign students increased. Unfortunately the programme was discontinued in 1968.

The international flavour created by the presence of students from many lands and cultures helped Canadians develop much broader perspectives with respect to their own problems. Canadians were surprised and impressed by how much the foreign students knew about Canada, its history, culture, and people, and how little they themselves knew about the countries from which these foreign students came. It was indeed a revealing experience.

Some years later, when I was working in the Caribbean, I met many of the former Labour College students. When I visited some in their homes, they were proud to show me their college graduation certificate, framed and hung in a prominent place.

Another interesting arrangement we made was a travel fellowship scheme. Before the inauguration of the college I approached a representative of the British Council, which stimulated cultural exchanges and provided scholarships for study in Britain. I enquired about the possibility of the council awarding travel scholarships to at least one French-speaking and one English-speaking student, who received the highest graduation mark in their respective classes. I explained that the purpose of the scholarships would be to have the winning students tour England and France for several weeks to study industrial relations and become acquainted with the labour movements of those countries.

The British Council representative liked the idea and said he believed arrangements for such a fellowship could be made. He undertook to discuss the proposal with the cultural attache of the French Embassy in order to ascertain their willingness to make this a joint British-French effort. One would be supported by the British Council to tour England for six weeks, and the other, supported by the French Embassy, to tour France for a similar period. I was delighted to make this announcement at the inauguration ceremonies. The first two scholarship winners were Jean Beaudry and Len Waller, both of the United Steelworkers. They travelled to Europe in fall 1963.

Many of our foreign students said their visits to various centres after the Labour College sessions were among the highlights of their stay in Canada. There they had the opportunity to visit industries, talk with management personnel, and meet with trade union leaders, as well as with members and their families. However, some students experienced less commendable situations. One student wrote about a Canadian union representative who accompanied his group as follows:

Eventually, we were in the city of Sault Ste. Marie with this representative. I could not allow his following remarks to go unheeded, for we had, for the previous four days, overlooked many similar remarks and, we being in the company of others at the time, feared that our continued silence and politeness might be understood. I quote his remarks: "Look at the state of Great Britain today, she is dragging her ass because of her generosity to Africa and those places to bring some sort of civility there. Let America, Britain and such countries pull out their investment in Africa and the West Indies and immediately these places will return to cannibalism."

Our foreign student had a proposal of how to deal with this matter:

In the light of this apparently poorly informed representative, I would wish to strongly recommend that he be given a stint at the Labour College of Canada, and placed in a room at the university campus between an African and a West Indian. His day-to-day association and discussion with the Colombo Plan students might, I hope, change his outlook.

The student's report continued with two more unfortunate examples. The first was a remark by the manager of a radio station:

How do you feel, having to adapt yourselves at short notice to the Canadian way of attire, especially having to wear shoes and be called upon to keep them on for the greater part of the day?

And the second came from an industrialist during a discussion on the invest-ment potentials of Trinidad and Tobago:

What part of Africa is Trinidad and Tobago?

But, apart from a few such "flea bites," the students' comments about these trips were very favourable.

In a group with such diverse backgrounds, problems and incidents were bound to arise. I want to mention only a few. One involved a Canadian who applied to attend the college two years in succession, and each year was turned down by the Labour College representative in his area on the ground that he did not have the academic qualifications to cope with the programme. When he applied the third year I was so impressed with his persistence that I argued with the Selection Committee in support of admitting him. In the end the committee reluctantly accepted the application. At the end of the term, when the student's final papers were marked, he failed to receive a passing mark. He tried, I know he did, but he just could not make the grade; it was beyond him. I never argued a similar case again.

Another time we had a case involving one of the foreign students. After his examination papers were marked it became clear that he did not pass, and so would not receive a graduation certificate. A day or two prior to the graduation ceremony I decided to inform him of the situation in order to avoid an unpleasant situation. I tried to explain, as gently as I could, but he seemed absolutely shattered. "But," he said, "I can't go back to my country without a diploma. I received so much publicity on being selected to come to Canada; how can I return a failure?"

He was emotionally shocked. What to do? I arranged to meet with professors who had marked his papers and I told them of my meeting with the student. The professors insisted that the marks were given in all honesty, and they had no wish to change them. I asked whether they would object to the student having a second try, but this time through an oral test which I would give. I know I did not fool them for a moment, but they agreed. On the morning of the graduation day I gave the student an oral test which lasted about an hour. In my judgement the student passed, and so he received his certificate.

There was another situation in the 1964 session which threatened to erupt into the open on graduation day. This involved the continued absence from classes of two students. When it became known that all students would receive graduation certificates, there was an undercurrent of protest by a number of the students, both Canadian and foreign. Some insisted that their protest be brought into the open at the time of the graduation ceremony. One foreign student who shared this view but did not want to create an unpleasant situation, described the resolution of the affair in these words:

An unpleasant situation in the presence of invited guests, press, radio and TV, was only avoided through the timely intervention and discussion by another Colombo Plan student and I, with others, over the days immediately prior to graduation day. We agreed on a compromise with the protesting students, whereby they would allow the graduation and presentation of certificates to come off without incident; and that they would bring their grievances to the attention of the Board of Governors of the Labour College and the Canadian Labour Congress in their respective reports. Whether they have, in fact, made mention of this in their reports I am not in a position to say. What I do know is that the graduation ceremonies went off without incident.

I was, of course, familiar with the problem, but I did not try to influence the students' planned action one way or the other. It was only when the students, staff, and guests were already gathered that I was informed of the compromise. I was proud of their wise and balanced decision, which I am sure was motivated by their deep interest and concern for the Labour College of Canada.

As in other similar institutions there were a number of incidents in the college, but most were pleasant and happy experiences. In the succeeding years the college continued to grow and improve and change, but it never lost sight of its mission, nor did it dilute the purpose for which it was established.

In 1969 I undertook a long-term assignment in Asia with the International Labour Organization, and I relinquished my post with the CLC. In 1977, when I was stationed in the Barbados, I received an invitation to attend the ceremonies marking the 15th anniversary of the college. I was happy to be invited, but also rather shocked to realize that so many years had passed so quickly. I arrived in Montreal the day before the event and returned to the Barbados the day after.

At McGill University there were only a few old timers who I knew, some were students of the 1960s and a few were CLC officials. The students of the 1977 term were a new generation of trade unionists. I felt almost lost in that familiar, yet so strange, environment as I sat on the platform and was introduced as the first registrar. Several speakers also referred to me kindly.

As I observed the ceremonies with deep nostalgia, I was sure that the interest and excitement which had prevailed at the inauguration of the college in 1963 was very much in evidence 15 years later. I also recalled an observation made to me at the inauguration by one of the students, and which I have often repeated. After he had received his certificate, and with distinction, I approached him and told him that I had clearance from the CLC to offer him the position of Congress education representative in Quebec. He was both surprised and pleased. He spoke to his wife, who was with him, and after a brief moment they jointly and happily agreed to accept our offer. After we agreed upon some details I asked: "Aren't you happy we found you here?" He did not reply for a moment, and then, with a distant look in his eyes, he said, "Brother Max, of course I am happy that I was found here, but I am much happier that here I found myself."

Is that not what the Labour College in Canada is all about?

ORGANIZED LABOUR is an integral part of Canadian society, and so it was only fitting that the CLC should have a place in the celebrations of the Centennial Year, marking the 100th anniversary of the Confederation of Canada. In summer 1964 the federal government invited organizations, including the CLC, to sponsor significant projects to mark the occasion. The Congress officers, in turn, asked departmental directors to submit ideas.

A thought which seemed appropriate had been germinating in my mind for some time, and I drafted a memorandum recommending that the Congress and the ICFTU jointly sponsor a World Conference on Labour Education during our Centennial Year. I suggested the conference be held in Montreal at the time of the World Fair, Expo '67. This, I felt, would be an additional attraction to delegates.

The memorandum dealt with the objectives and administrative details and I asked authorization to invite the ICFTU to participate. Executive Vice-President Joe Morris informed me that the officers approved the project in principle, though they were naturally anxious to know the extent of the Congress' financial obligation. While I was unable to provide figures, I assured him I was confident, very confident, that the greater part of the budget could be raised in Canada. I felt he was more impressed with my enthusiasm for the conference than with my assurance that we could meet a significant share of the cost; but, in any event, I was authorized to approach the ICFTU.

I wrote Herbert A. Tulatz, the Assistant General Secretary at Brussels, outlining the proposal. In due course the Executive Board of that organization gave its approval, accepting our invitation and instructing the ICFTU secretariat to proceed with the necessary arrangements. The sum of $73,500 was set aside from the Solidarity Fund as the ICFTU's maximum contribution, on the understanding that this amount was to be reduced by funds raised by the CLC and a contribution from the ILO, which together had been estimated at $30,000.

In August 1965 Tulatz came to Ottawa to discuss the general composition of the conference, its scope, aims, finances, and a host of other matters. It was agreed that:

1) The conference would be held in Montreal, 16-26 August 1967.

2) The number of participants would not exceed 200.

3) Participants would be trade union officials responsible for labour education in their own unions, directors of labour colleges, and representatives from international agencies, such as the ILO and UNESCO.

4) The conference would be conducted in four languages (English, French, Spanish, and German), with simultaneous translation.

5) Tulatz and I would be co-directors. In the main he would oversee all sessions, as well as approach international agencies for financial support. I would be responsible for all technical and financial arrangements, including the solicitation

of funds from Canadian sources.

Arrangements were finalized at a meeting in Brussels, 30 March 1966, attended by a number of European education consultants. The aims of the conference were also defined. They were:

1) To examine and evaluate labour education programmes of the free trade union movement in light of the significant and rapidly — changing technological, economic, and political conditions.

2) To discuss ways and means for increasing the allocation of resources for educational activities.

3) To formulate broad policies for encouraging and convincing governments, international agencies, and the general public of the constructive and essential role that labour education plays in national development.

After the Brussels meeting I became involved in a myriad of technical and financial responsibilities. This, of course, was in addition to my duties as Director of Education, Registrar of the Labour College, and as a member of a number of committees. My life was full of interesting and exciting activities, but to complicate the situation still further, in the summer of 1966 I was about to become involved in an ICFTU assignment in Trinidad and Tobago. This was to eventually lead to a significant change in my life, that of my family, and in my career.

Early in August 1967, I took a month off from this assignment to return to Montreal and take part in the World Conference. There were some 299 delegates from 60 countries. Many of the Asian and African delegates were in their traditional multi-coloured costumes. At the back of the platform was a large mural, designed by the CLC's own artist, the late Harry Kelman. This graphically illustrated the solidarity and vitality of the world labour movement. It was an inspiring spectacle with a truly international atmosphere.

Herbert Tulatz, as Chairman of the plenary sessions, opened the conference with a thoughtful and challenging address. He said the conference marked a turning point for the tradition-bound labour movement; labour education had to prepare trade unionists for the technical age. He expressed the hope that the conference would stimulate a broadening of the aims and methods of education in light of labour's increasing role and responsibility in influencing economic and social policies.

CLC Executive Vice-President Joe Morris urged the delegates to welcome and propagate new ideas. The labour movement, he reminded them, was founded on principles that were often not generally accepted. Unions in both developed and underdeveloped countries needed to improve their capacity and ability to play their new role in society effectively.

There were a number of other speakers. Bernard Tacks, Vice-President of the West German Trade Union Federation (DGB), spoke of the need for greater emphasis on labour solidarity and the inclusion of political issues in educational programmes. Peter Rosenfeld, Educational Officer of the British Union of Distributive and Allied Workers, read a thoughtful paper on the necessity of preparing for such responsibilities. His presentation led to considerable discussion.

Walter G. Davis, AFL-CIO Educational Director, reported on increased political activity on the part of the labour movement in the United States. The AFL-CIO had played a decisive role in the passage of the American Civil Rights Act in 1964. Manuel Penalver, press officer of the Venezuelan Confederation of Workers (CTV), gave an overview of the difficult political conditions unions were facing in many Latin American countries. In some their survival as free associations was tenuous. His own union, however, was growing and was giving high priority to labour education, stressing programmes that trained and encouraged workers to participate more fully in social and economic affairs.

Kalmen Kaplansky, Director of the ILO's Canadian Office, said the full utilization of human resources was the most important, pressing, and decisive issue for economic development.

The delegates were divided into five working groups for detailed discussion of various aspects of both labour and public education. Each group reported its findings and recommendations to the plenary sessions. After these reports were discussed, and in some cases amended, they formed the general consensus of the conference, which might be summarized as follows:

1) That national labour movements make every effort to increase their resources for labour education.

2) That labour education officers re-examine their programmes with a view to making them more relevant to changing economic and social conditions.

3) That education programmes include specialized training for union representatives on various public bodies; and for active involvement in political affairs, without compromising the independent status of the labour movement.

4) That free public education be made available to all people in all countries; and that vocational education be broadened to include training in the fundamentals of a number of related jobs within a trade.

5) That unions make every effort to include in their agreements provision for educational leave with pay.

In my remarks at the closing session I tried to relate the broad objectives of the conference to the discussions and recommendations of the delegates. I felt that, while the conference had succeeded in meeting its objectives, conferences and resolutions did not in themselves effect changes and improvements. There was a need for labour leaders to elevate education to a higher priority. I suggested that in countries which received United Nations assistance for their economic development, unions should press more vigorously for the inclusion of allocations for labour education as an element for achieving economic development. I also told the delegates that, through the experiences of some foreign students participating in our Canadian programmes, I had learned the importance of designing and constructing programmes in the context of local conditions. These students had found it difficult to apply or adapt Canadian problems to those prevailing in their home localities. This lesson was being reinforced by my experiences in the Caribbean.

The conference adjourned on a note of satisfaction and high expectation for the future development of labour education.

CHAPTER TWELVE

International Assignments

VIVID IMPRESSIONS of the first ILO Conference I attended in Geneva in 1952 have remained with me through the years, though I little knew at the time how deeply they would later relate to my life and career. This was the largest such conference ever held, 700 delegates from 60 countries, many in flowing colourful native dress. They talked in many languages of how to improve the living and working conditions of people throughout the world. It was a new sensation and I felt as though I was intimately surrounded by the whole world.

The Canadian delegation reflected the tripartite nature of the ILO, namely representative of government, employers, and labour. M.M. MacLean, Assistant Deputy Minister of Labour, and Paul Goulet, Assistant to the Deputy Minister and Director of the ILO branch, were the government nominees. Harry Taylor represented the Canadian Manufacturers' Association, and I was the labour delegate.

Paul Goulet, a very efficient yet kindly person, helped me in an almost fatherly fashion to understand better the nature of the ILO, its programmes, and the issues that would come before the conference. He also told me that, while it was not mandatory, it was customary for delegates to address the general session on the report of the Director General, who at that time was David Morse. If I wished to speak, I should submit my name in advance. Having never before declined an invitation to speak, I seized the opportunity, rather surprising Goulet with my haste.

For several nights I worked, carefully preparing my speech. Finally my turn came, and when my name was called I suddenly became quite nervous, remaining in my place for several long seconds. When my name was called the second time, I got up and during the long walk to the rostrum the tension eased.

I have a record of my address. In part I said:

> I regret that the Report gives little cause for rejoicing insofar as present world conditions are concerned. It is indeed, sad to read the following lines in the introduction to the Report: "I would like to be able to say that the world is in a better condition today than it was a year ago, that the danger of war has been eliminated, that the devotion of vast resources to rearmament has ended, and that nations are able to give all their attention to overcoming the real enemies of man: poverty, ignorance, disease and inhuman living conditions. Unfortunately, this is not the case.
>
> Unfortunately indeed; and yet, while this is the actual situation, reality is not without hope, and hope is not without optimism. Nations are still discussing their differences, and as long as they are sitting around the table, engaged in what we call collective bargaining, there may yet come about lasting collective security.

I then went on to talk about economic conditions in Canada.

When the conference ended I have become convinced that Canadian workers should know more about the ILO, and that we, as labour educators, could do something about this. However, it was some time before we introduced discussion on the ILO into the TLC's educational programme, and even then our efforts were not very productive. We just did not know how to relate the objectives and work of the ILO to the concerns and interests of Canadian workers in a manner that would be both interesting and meaningful.

Another opportunity for me to learn about the ILO came in 1958 when the ILO and the Asian Labour Education Centre of the University of the Philippines arranged a joint conference on labour education to be held in the Philippines. I was invited to participate. This was a valuable experience, enabling me to learn more about the technical aspects of the organization's activities, and to become acquainted with the labour movement and its leaders in that part of the world.

I was a great admirer of Prime Minister Jawaharlal Nehru of India, and, before I left Canada, I tried to arrange through the Department of External Affairs to make a courtesy call on Nehru after the conference ended. About a week after I arrived in the Philippines I was advised that such arrangements had been made. As this was simply a courtesy call, our discussion was by no means epic, but one thing he said has remained with me ever since. Referring to a number of rather serious strikes then taking place in India, he commented: "You know, I certainly agree that all workers should have the right to strike." He paused, and then with a slight sigh added: "But I wish they would not exercise that right so often in India."

Then, in 1960, there came an excellent opportunity to explore methods of teaching workers about the ILO. The United Nations Educational, Scientific and Cultural Organization (UNESCO) announced a World Conference on Adult Education to be held in Montreal in October 1960. I anticipated that a number of labour educators from the United States and Canada would attend, as well as representatives from the ILO. I thought they would most likely be prepared to spend a few additional days at a workshop to discuss and design an ILO teaching programme.

After clearing the idea with the Congress officers and the National Education Advisory Committee, I wrote Albert Guigui, chief of the ILO's Industrial Workers' Division, with the suggestion. He replied that the ILO was happy to accept the invitation to be a joint sponsor with the CLC. The workshop was held at St. Agathe des Monts with 35 participants and five observers. Ways and means of conveying information about the ILO were discussed. This was the first venture of its kind in the history of the ILO Workers' Education Programme, and it appeared to meet a need. While the ILO's activities in this field were mainly devoted to the developing countries, the workshop provided an opportunity to meet some of the workers' educational needs in industrially-advanced countries and led the way to similar programmes in other areas of the world.

This resulted in improvements in our teaching methods and the creating of greater interest in the ILO. "Teaching Workers About the ILO" became a regular feature in the ILO's programme.

In 1965 I attended an ILO international meeting of labour education consultants and was honoured in being elected chairman.

Autumn 1966 marked the beginning of a still deeper involvement in ILO affairs, one that eventually led to significant changes in my life. Earlier that year John

Simonds, a CLC Vice-President, had gone to Trinidad and Tobago on a mission for ICFTU. The labour movement there was seriously divided and in disarray. Simonds had been asked to assist in trying to effect improvements.

During his stay the Minister of Labour and some of the union leaders told him of their plans to establish a labour college. They had asked the ILO to designate a person to undertake the project, but no name had been forthcoming. Simonds told them of my work in establishing the Labour College of Canada and suggested I would be a suitable person, if satisfactory arrangements could be made. As a result of these discussions, I received an invitation from the ILO to undertake the assignment. After some exchanges of correspondence between the ILO and the CLC I was granted a year's leave of absence. Some of my Congress duties were, meantime, to be assumed by Link Bishop, the CLC's Educational Director in Ontario.

I arrived in Port-of-Spain, the capital of Trinidad and Tobago, 19 August 1966, and the following day met with Jim Adams, the Permanent Secretary to the Minister of Labour, similar to our Deputy Minister. I was pleasantly surprised to learn that the framework for a college had already been established. A committee, representative of government, labour, and employers, had been at work examining ways and means for developing labour education activities on a more organized and permanent basis.

Their recommendations included:

1) That a permanent labour education centre be established and named the Cipriani Labour College. (Arthur Andrew Cipriani, 1875-1945, was one of the nation's early crusaders for social justice and enlightened legislation.)

2) That the objectives of the College be to provide trade union training and workers' education, to conduct courses, seminars, and other such activities in the field of industrial relations, and to undertake research into problems affecting labour and industrial relations.

3) That a Board of Governors be established, consisting of five representatives of the trade union movement; the Permanent Secretary to the Minister of Labour; the Permanent Secretary to the Minister of Education and Culture; a representative of the University of the West Indies; and two public-spirited citizens selected by the government, one of whom to be chairman.

4) That the government provide the basic funds for the operation of the College.

5) That an official request be made to the ILO to assign a labour education specialist to assist in the technicalities and details that had to be worked out before the College could become operational.

With these basic decisions agreed upon, my first responsibility was to design the programme, engage teaching staff, and obtain reading material for the students. I considered it helpful to identify the social framework within which the programme would be developed. I listed the following principles:

1) That the trade unions constitute an integral part of democratic society, and that their existence and development is socially desirable.

2) That collective bargaining is a logical and effective process in a free democracy.

3) That conflict of interest between employers and workers can be harmonized by mature and well-informed management and unions, particularly where they are assisted by enlightened labour legislation.

4) That industry, both private and public, must operate efficiently and profitably.

5) That the interests of management and labour must be compatible with the interests of all, and that both have responsibilities to the nation.

In order to carry out these principles an academic programme was prepared consisting of two two-month day courses, two five-month evening courses, eight two-week day courses and 18 weekend schools throughout the country. These courses were conducted at various levels of union responsibility.

The subject material included Labour's role and activities in economic development, basic economics, industrial relations, labour legislation in the Caribbean, writing a collective agreement, Caribbean and world labour history, and instructor training.

The Board of Governors readily accepted this approach and, after a series of meetings, the College began to take shape. It opened 19 October 1966, two months after my arrival. I had become very impressed with the kindness and co-operation of many people in all sectors of society. The press reported favourable on our efforts, and it seemed everyone supported us and wished us well. This kindness and attention and the natural beauty of this tropical country influenced my somewhat-romanticized but factual account of the opening including a report I sent to the ILO headquarters, describing the scene:

The stately old house in a quiet, elite residential area of Port-of-Spain was ceremoniously decorated and freshly painted in soft azure, coral and yellow. Under the shade of a twisted avocado tree, rooted in the centre of the manicured lawn, a band dressed in gay uniforms, played familiar tunes.

Inside some 200 people crowded the building to its limits. As the Prime Minister, the Right Honourable Dr. Eric Williams, and the Governor General, Sir Solomon Hocher, arrived in their shiny black limousines, they were greeted by a white-helmeted guard of honour. It was a colourful spectacle.

The Prime Minister delivered the inaugural address, saying in part:

As I declare open this College to the memory of Captain Arthur Cipriani, let us hope that from it will come men and women educated in the requirements of good trade union membership and disciplined and efficient leadership, so that they may be better able to play their part in overcoming the problems which confront us as we seek the social and economic betterment of the nation.

The Cipriani Labour College was formally launched.

During my work in Trinidad and Tobago I came to know all the labour leaders in the country. Two of them, Daniel Critchlow and Selbin John, were the presidents of separate public employees' unions. I thought it was unfortunate that, in such a small country, there should be two unions in the same field, and, although I realized this was far beyond my terms of reference, I decided to try to bring them together.

First, I spoke to the two presidents separately about the idea of a merger. Each said he would be quite happy with such a move, but neither wanted to take the initiative. I suggested I would be glad to preside over a small unpublicized meeting of the organizations. They agreed and shortly afterward I convened a meeting of the three top officers of each of the organizations. It was evident from our first discussion that the possibility of a merger was there, although there remained the question of assignment of officers and staff. We continued the discussions for several weeks, during which time the matter of a constitution arose. I undertook to assist in the drafting; but this proved more difficult than I anticipated. On more than one occasion, one or the other union walked out a meeting because of disagreement. And, in fact, as chairman of the committee, I also walked out on occasion, telling the representatives that, unless they were more serious about the merger, I would have nothing more to do with it.

In due course, agreement was reached. The discussions had been conducted secretly, because we did not want to give publicity to matters that were still under discussion. However, before the matters were finalized, and before we were ready to give publicity to our talks, the *Daily Chronicle* learned about our meetings and gave the matter full coverage. The article referred to "an expatriate, who initiated the unity move." It was, of course, known that I was the "expatriate," but for some reason I was not named.

Shortly after a convention was arranged, and the two public employees' unions merged, becoming the largest trade union in the country. When I visited Trinidad and Tobago in 1977, I was pleased to find the union doing exceedingly well. The government, however, was annoyed with me for assisting in uniting the two unions, and my contract was not extended for another period, as had originally been planned. Nevertheless, I was delighted in playing a part in the merger. A month later I undertook a mission to Guyana, with a view to establishing a labour college there.

While I was in Trinidad and Tobago I had been visited by the Secretary of the Trade Union Council of Guyana, J.H. Pollydore. He wanted to learn about the structure, programme, and funding of the Cipriani Labour College. He told me that about two years earlier they had established a labour institute in Guyana. It was named after Nat Critchlow, a former waterfront worker, labour leader, and political crusader. Administered by the Trade Union Council, it was funded mainly by the American Institute for Free Labour Development (AIFLD), a body established by the AFL-CIO in the early 1960s to develop workers' educational activities through programmes financed by the United States government. I did not take seriously rumours that some of this funding came from the Central Intelligence Agency.

Pollydore said that, for a variety of reasons, the Critchlow Institute had not been able to develop an effective programme, and he wondered whether, when I finished my assignment in Trinidad and Tobago, I would be interested in going to Guyana to assist them. I quickly assured him that I would be interested, but arrangements would have to be made with the ILO and the CLC. I was not too optimistic about this possibility, but Pollydore seemed to know how to go about it. After various exchanges of correspondence, arrangements were completed and it was agreed that I would assume my new post in Guyana in September 1967.

At Georgetown, the capital of Guyana, I moved into a rambling old house built on stilts by the sea, where my wife later joined me. Within a few days of my arrival discussions began with trade union and government officials as to how best to reshape and redirect the Critchlow Labour Institute. People were most co-operative and supportive. Among them were the Minister of Labour and Social Services, the Honourable Claude A. Merryman, his Permanent Secretary, F.G. Taharally, the President and Secretary of the Trade Union Council, Richard Ishmawl, and Joseph Pollydore.

I wanted to know what they regarded as the weaknesses and shortcomings of the Institute, what their expectations were, and how the programme could be improved. From my Trinidad and Tobago experience I was well aware of the sensitivity of the people involved, and I directed my attention to the future, rather than the past. Soon our talks identified concrete objectives and plans for a recon-structed labour education centre. We prepared new by-laws with a preamble which called for a broadening of the administration through the involvement of represen-tatives from the government, the University of Guyana, the public and others. The academic programme was to be conducted on two levels, elementary and advanced, with courses ranging from weekend seminars in areas outside Georgetown, to a two-month full-time course at the College.

We decided to carry on with the courses already planned and begin the new programme with a two-month course commencing in January 1968. Meanwhile there was a great deal of preparatory work to be done: selecting teaching staff, obtaining text books, preparing course outlines, recruiting and screening students, engaging office staff, and a host of other things. The three fundamental and most-urgent matters were obtaining adequate funds, appointing a principal, and finding a suitable home for the College.

On the matter of finance, the government agreed to increase its contribution from $10,000 a year to $25,000, and the Trade Union Council undertook to increase its financial contribution substantially. The appointment of a principal was left to a later date, while I was asked to assume the immediate responsibility of that position. Without requesting the ILO for authorization to act in such a capacity, which I should have done, I accepted.

The matter of quarters was more complicated. We were meeting in a small Transport Workers' Union hall in an antiquated waterfront building, reminiscent of some Canadian labour temples of the 1930s. On one occasion I met with Pollydore and George DePeane, on whom I often relied for advice and assistance. DePeane was a competent and enthusiastic young labour leader who was very popular, and who became a highly respected ILO representative in the Caribbean. At this meeting I asked where the new College was to be housed. I was told: "Here." I found it hard to believe — the room was far too small and, rather impatiently I'm afraid, I said bluntly that it simply would not do.

Slowly, quietly, and I suspect rather sadly, Pollydore said: "But, Brother Max, this is the only space we have."

I undertook to discuss the matter with the Minister of Labour. When I did he explained to me that the government's own ministries were scattered in old houses around the city, and the government was in no position to provide permanent facilities for the College. There was, however, a house assigned to one ministry that was not in use, and that could be made available to the College for a six-month period. I quickly accepted, and so the College began its activities in quarters that were reasonably adequate, but definitely temporary.

One day, as I was scouting the city for a more permanent home, I came across a large vacant lot opposite a new technical school. As I stood looking at the land where cows and sheep were grazing, I imagined I saw a beautiful complex of buildings rising from the tall grass, a new home for the labour movement of Guyana and the Critchlow Labour College. I thought that, with careful planning and considerable effort, the dream might be realized.

The first step was to obtain the endorsement of the Trade Union Council. When I met with the officers I outlined the proposal, not forgetting to say that the accommodation would be for both the College and the Trade Union Council. Their reaction was almost predictable. Thinking that I could get the money from the ILO or some other such source they were momentarily delighted. But, when I explained that I could not possible do that, their mood changed.

I said that, in my opinion, if the project were to be realized, it should be a truly Guyanese effort, designed by a Guyanese architect, built by Guyanese workers, using as much indigenous material as possible, and financed by the people of Guyana. Seeing the doubtful expression on the faces of some of the officers, I quickly added that I would undertake to raise some of the money from outside sources and would participate in a financial drive in Guyana.

I think my somewhat impassioned presentation impressed most of the officers, but Winslow Carrington of the Transport Workers' Union, who later became Minister of Labour, had serious doubts. He spoke to me in an almost fatherly manner: "Brother Max, I certainly appreciate your enthusiasm; but you have been here only a few weeks. You don't know this country well. Most of our people are very poor, and raising money here, even for such a worthy cause as the Critchlow Labour College, would be very difficult. I tell you, my good brother, the effort may very well break your heart."

I could not resist the temptation, giving what I believed was an appropriate reply, even if it were a bit dramatic: "Brother Carrington, trying to raise money for the Critchlow building and not succeeding will not, I assure you, break my heart; but not trying at all may."

I went on to say that I was somewhat familiar with the government's efforts to encourage Guyanese people to undertake "self-help" projects, several of which had recently been reported in the press. The Critchlow Labour College campaign would definitely be in that category. Finally the TUC officers agreed to endorse and support a campaign to raise funds.

The next step was a meeting with an architect. George Henry was a talented and imaginative young Guyanese who had been trained in England. I went to see him and told him our need, explaining that we had no funds to commence construction, nor even to pay him. I added that I was unable even to give assurance that he would be the chosen architect, for this was a decision for the Board of Governors. His handsome face broke into a broad smile, and he asked: "Mr. Swerdlow, what do I get out of this if I make the initial plans and not get the job?"

"If that happens George, I assure you that you will have the eternal gratitude of the saints in heaven," I replied.

He bent over his desk and laughed heartily for a long time. When he straightened up he spoke: "You know Max, in the years I have been a professional architect, no one has offered me a deal such as you have. I can't possibly refuse you."

George Henry and I became good friends the first time we met. In the months that followed we spent a great deal of time together, at all hours of the day and night, planning, dreaming, and arguing about designs. We agreed that, as this was the first project of its kind in the history of Guyana, it should not just meet our educational requirements, but should also be a thing of beauty.

While he was working on his drawings, I turned my attention to obtaining the land, which was Crown property. I knew the Minister of Labour, Claude Merryman, quite well and asked him to arrange a meeting with the Prime Minister, Forbes Burnham. At the same time I asked George Henry for some preliminary plans.

When we met I spread the multi-coloured drawing across the Prime Minister's desk, saying: "Mr. Prime Minister, you give us the land and we will give you this building." He looked at the plans for a long time, as though he was examining every square inch. He seemed impressed with both the design and our confidence; and turning to Pollydore, said he saw no great difficulty, but he would have to determine whether there were other plans for the property.

Then he turned to me: "Mr. Swerdlow, I see this building plan includes the construction of a cafeteria, is that justified? Would the Labour College have sufficient students to justify the construction and maintenance of a cafeteria?"

I knew that, sooner or later, someone would ask that question, but I did not anticipate it from the Prime Minister. I was grateful he raised it because I felt I had an ace up my sleeve.

"Mr. Prime Minister," I said, "the number of students in the College would, perhaps, not justify the cost of a cafeteria; but right across the road is your technical school, with an enrolment of more than 300 students, and there is not cafeteria of any kind there, or even nearby. Is it not realistic to assume that many of those students would be happy to walk across the road to our cafeteria? This is one of the reasons we hope to get this property. If we do, it would be good for our College and for your technical school."

The Prime Minister laughed and made a slight bow, as if acknowledging good planning. After a few drinks of rum and ginger we left. A few days later Pollydore received a message from the Prime Minister's office saying the land was ours.

Now it was time to begin raising money for actual construction. As this was to be a labour centre it was only reasonable to expect the unions to be the first to make substantial contributions; but the Trade Union Council did not have "substantial funds." To overcome this difficulty we devised a plan that was far more effective than a cheque from the TUC. George Henry designed a certificate with an architectural sketch of the College, and an inscription saying that the holder of the certificate had contributed at least one dollar toward the construction of the building.

We printed 50,000, one for each member of the trade union movement in Guyana, and every union took as many certificates as it had members. These were sold in factories, offices, and the field; and members proudly displayed them in their homes. Thus, the Trade Union Council fulfilled its commitment, raising $50,000. Equally important, union members were made to feel, in a very real sense, that they had made a contribution to the construction of a new home for their labour movement.

An important factor in fund-raising was keeping the public informed, and I established a good relationship with the city editor of the country's only daily newspaper, *The Daily Graphic*. Accounts of our progress appeared regularly.

The next step was to approach industry for contributions. We realized that a good selling point would be a provision enabling companies to write off their contributions for tax purposes because the College was an educational undertaking. Through the Minister of Finance this was arranged, and a public announcement was made that contributions to the Critchlow Labour College would be tax deductible.

I then planned to approach the Demerara Bauxite Company, the country's largest industry, which was a subsidiary of the Aluminum Company of Canada (ALCAN). R.E. Powell, Chairman of the Labour College of Canada, was a director of ALCAN, and so I telephoned him in Montreal. I told him briefly of our campaign and my intention to approach Demerara for a contribution. I asked if he would be willing to use his influence with the company to ensure we received a "substantial" contribution. After a moment of silence, he characteristically asked: "What do you want?" I quickly replied: "Ten thousand dollars." Again there was silence, and then he asked when I was seeing the company. I asked when I should; and with a chuckle he suggested, "two or three days." I thanked him and when I met the Demerara officials I had little difficulty obtaining a cheque for $10,000, especially as it was tax-deductible.

The momentum of our drive was increasing almost daily. I visited as many companies as I could, large and small, and accepted contributions of cash or building materials. Cash donations went from $100 all the way up to $45,000. The government had not only contributed land, but had also provided a large quantity of lumber from its own sawmill. Other contributions of building material included 100 feet of galvanized pipe, 3,500 bags of cement, $10,000 worth of lumber, $4,000 worth of paint, windows, electrical fixtures, and many similar materials.

The largest contribution received, and one which displayed a good deal of business acumen, was $45,000 from Banks Breweries, earmarked to cover the cost of the cafeteria. I thought that, as the cafeteria would serve beer, among other beverages, Banks was a logical company to approach for a sizable contribution. Armed with a complete set of plans I arranged to meet the owner and general manager, Peter D'Aguir. He was impressed with the plans and assured me his company would make a contribution. I said I not only hoped for a contribution, I hoped the company would finance the $45,000 cost of the cafeteria.

He seemed surprised, and said a donation of that proportion would set a dangerous precedent for appeals from other institutions. I pointed out the goodwill and favourable publicity that would result and said the company's support would be permanently recorded by a plaque on the cafeteria wall. Finally, I pointed out that the workers were the brewery's best customers.

He then said that the final decision would rest with the company's Board of Directors, and that he would place our request before the directors.

"Will you personally support our request?" I asked.

"I am quite sympathetic, but I must think a little more about the implications of this kind of a commitment," he said.

I felt this was not too reassuring, and asked if I might appear before the Board. I was surprised at how quickly he agreed.

When the day came the meeting was held in a small, unpretentious, and smoke-filled room at the brewery. When I entered I had a feeling that the matter had already been discussed. I gave some background information on the College, its programme, and its contribution to labour-management relations in Guyana. I explained our need for suitable facilities and our plans for the future. The ten or twelve men around the table listened politely and attentively. I then unrolled the architectural plans on the table, saying: "Gentlemen, this is the cafeteria I am asking you to build."

They looked at the plans with evident interest, and then one of the directors spoke: "Mr. Swerdlow, as you know, we are a business firm. Good will and publicity, as you say, is important to us, but do you really believe we could get more publicity and goodwill if we gave $45,000 rather than the $10,000 as the Demerara Bauxite Company gave you?"

Momentarily, I was hard-pressed for a reply to what seemed like a logical question. Then an idea sparked my mind. "Sir, of course you are a business concern; then I will make you a business proposition. You give us the $45,000 and in return I will give you an agreement from the Critchlow Labour College that for the first five years the cafeteria is open no other than Banks beer will be sold there."

There was dead silence in the room. The directors had not expected a business proposition, and frankly I had not gone to the meeting with one. I was asked to wait outside while they discussed the proposal. About half an hour later I was called in, and I immediately knew, from their smiling faces, that the proposition had been accepted. I was told that this was the case, and formal details would be worked out.

I was confident that I would have no difficulty getting the five-year commitment from the College. Although different brands of beer were imported, Banks was the only brewing company in Guyana, and its employees were members of the trade union movement. When I returned to Guyana in 1977, some eight years later, Banks beer was still the only brand sold in the cafeteria.

By January 1968, some three months after we began our financial campaign, we had commitments for cash or building materials amounting to about $200,000, roughly two-thirds of the estimated total cost. On 2 February we had a ground-breaking ceremony.

Plans for the complex included: five administrative offices, two of which would be for the Trade Union Council; three classrooms; a students' common room; the cafeteria, with seating for 100; a library; a dormitory to accommodate 40 students; and an auditorium to seat about 350. The auditorium was to be the show-piece of the complex. I encouraged George Henry to give his talent full freedom, and he did. The room was circular, with a high cathedral-like ceiling and massive exposed steel rafters painted black. Part of the wall was all glass, with doors opening on an inner courtyard. Opposite was a wall built of a variety of carefully-selected Guyana hardwoods. The auditorium was intended to be a multi-purpose room, available for conferences, theatrical performances, and other cultural activities. Thus the facilities would extend well beyond our purely labour-educational needs and would contribute significantly to the life of the whole community.

Arrangements with a local building contractor were completed in early June, but before he took possession, we arranged a symbolic ceremony marking our "self-help" efforts. Students from the College, with some other trade unionists, brought picks and shovels and started digging trenches for the foundation of the first building. Our two days of voluntary work gained us a great deal of newspaper publicity as well as effecting some savings.

Naturally, progress in the construction was not without its difficulties. Sometimes material was not delivered on time, or key tradesmen were not immediately available, or the architect was not on hand. At one point there was a dispute between the contractor and his employees over the matter of overtime. It was settled when we agreed to make additional money available to meet the workers' demands. Despite all this, the workers knew the purpose of the project and they worked hard and conscientiously, so progress was steady.

But there was one incident that nearly destroyed our whole undertaking and threatened to shatter our dream. Soon after construction commenced, I had occasion to go to Jamaica for a few days to attend a conference. When I returned, my wife and the government's chief conciliation officer were at the airport to meet me. As we drove home my wife told me there was "some bad news," but that I should not get too upset. She explained: "Someone has given a story to the press saying that there was a fraud of $7,000 at the Critchlow Labour College. The police are investigating and have seized all the books and financial records from Pollydore."

It had been front page news in the *Daily Graphic*. At first I was shocked, and then angry. Disregarding the hours of the night, as soon as we arrived home I began telephoning, but no one knew where the story originated.

Early the next morning the Chief of Police telephoned, asking if he could come to my home to discuss the matter. I was most anxious to talk to him, and a short time later he arrived, a tall, handsome black man, with curly white hair. He immediately told me that I was not a suspect. I almost choked on the coffee I was drinking, and told him with obvious sarcasm that I was greatly relieved. He said he expected the investigation would be completed within a few days and our records would then be returned. I tried to be as polite and self-composed as I could, but it was difficult.

Our conversation went something like this: "Chief, is it customary for your department to launch a formal investigation in such cases?"

"Normally, perhaps not," he said; "but this case is different. You see the Critchlow Labour College has been soliciting money and building supplies from public institutions, and when someone alleges that such funds were improperly or fraudulently used, it is our duty to investigate."

"Could you tell me who made the charges?"

"No."

"Then any Tom, Dick or Harry can telephone the police and make unfounded allegations and you at once begin an investigation?"

He looked at me, as though he was sending me a message: "Mr. Swerdlow, it is not quite as simple as you make it out to be. I assure you the allegations in this case were not made by a Tom, a Dick or a Harry. When a well-known person makes that kind of a charge we have to investigate. Don't you see?"

I had a feeling that he had slipped, accidentally or intentionally. "A well-known person" was the first indication we had as to who might have made the allegations, but there was still nothing tangible to go by. We turned our attention to trying to remedy the damage that had been done.

We held an emergency meeting of the College Board of Governors. Pollydore reported that, with the exception of one lump sum cheque to the contractor, there had been no payments made from the fund. No one had any idea who started the rumour, or where the $7,000 figure came from. The Board issued a public statement declaring:

> We can only assume that an unwarranted and malicious statement was made by a most irresponsible person who is not connected with the College, but who motivated the police investigation and false sensational reports in the press.
>
> It is understandable that the public, and particularly those who have so generously contributed to the College, should become concerned. We again categorically deny the alleged fraud of $7,000 in the light of what we know, and can only hope that the irresponsibility which caused this development will not mar public confidence in the College. If it does, the nation will ultimately be the loser. We are determined not to let this happen.

At my request *The Daily Graphic* gave the statement the same front page prominence it had given the original report. We also engaged a chartered accountant to prepare a detailed financial statement which was made public and sent to all contributors. In a few days the police returned our books with a brief statement saying their investigation had shown the charges to be unsubstantiated and false.

The eventual explanation would have been humorous, had the affair not been so serious. It appeared that a high-ranking government official was doing some construction work at his home, and late one evening he visited our building site and helped himself to seven bags of cement. The night watchman told someone about the incident. This someone told someone else, who told someone else, and so on. By the time the story reached the person who made the false charges, the seven bags of cement had become $7,000.

Soon the affair was forgotten, and no longer talked about. I realized, for the first time, why the ILO did not like their representatives to become involved in financial campaigns, and after Guyana I never did so again.

By early July 1968, my assignment had only three months to go. We were making good progress without academic programmes, but I regretted that much of the building construction was not going to be completed before it was time for me to leave. The Minister of Labour raised the possibility of a one-year extension assignment. I told him I would be more than delighted, but it depended on the ILO and the CLC. He said he would approach the ILO, and I undertook to write the CLC. I sent the congress a report of our activities and asked for both an extension of my leave of absence and a $5,000 contribution to the College. In due course I received both the extension and the cheque.

By October 1969, the administration building, with its classrooms, offices, and a common room, was completed and we moved from the temporary location to our permanent home. There were some continuing problems with construction, but, one way or another, we managed to overcome them.

There was, however, an unexpected personal development when I received a letter from Paul Chu, Chief of the Workers' Education Branch of the ILO, asking if I would be interested in a three-year assignment in Asia. My wife and I discussed the offer for hours and hours, because there were so many unanswered questions. The prospect was exciting and challenging, but I could hardly expect the Canadian Labour Congress to grant a further leave of absence. I was already 50 years of age, and if I left the Congress and the ILO assignment terminated after three years, I would be in a difficult position. Above all there was the consideration of my family.

Eventually I went to Geneva to discuss the matter, and, as a result, received a letter from the ILO stating that, providing funds were available at the conclusion of the three-year term, my contract would be extended for further two years. On that basis I accepted th offer, with the provision that I would remain in Guyana until at least May, when I expected most of the building contracts would be completed.

From Geneva I flew to Canada for a few days, to explain my situation to the Congress. I admitted I was taking a chance, but Bill Dodge, then the Secretary-Treasurer, assured me that if my ILO contract was not extended past three years, the Congress would feel obligated to re-employ me in some capacity. I was greatly relieved by this friendly and generous attitude.

Back in Guyana another problem had been solved when Dr. Harold Brotman, a most dedicated and competent young man, accepted the position of acting principal of the College.

Once, as I stood in the entrance hall that led to the auditorium, I noticed a blank wall, some thirty feet in length and ten feet in height. It occurred to me that this would be an ideal location for a colourful mural. I discussed the idea with George Henry, who responded with his unusual enthusiasm, and with some of the Governors. There was general support, and agreement that a suitable theme would be the history of the labour movement in Guyana. We decided to hold a contest for the design and execution by a Guyanese artist. A committee including media and university people was appointed to act as judges, and we received five submissions.

I think I had assumed the artist finally chosen would be a black male. However, the unanimous choice was Leila Locke, a young white Englishwoman who was married to a black Guyanese. We discussed her fee, which she set at $2,000, with the College providing the necessary scaffolding. This could have been financed by the College, but we decided instead to approach one of the country's leading retailers, T. Gebdes Grant, a company we had not approached in our earlier financial campaign. The company readily agreed to cover the cost of the mural.

Leila Locke was a quiet, unassuming, tireless artist. She usually worked in the evening, after the construction crew had left, often continuing until midnight. I sometimes watched her, and was fascinated by their technique. Gradually the images emerged, resembling the powerful figures seen in the paintings of Orosco, the great Mexican painter. Six weeks later we were able to stand back and admire Mrs. Locke's graphic painting. Telling, as it does, the history of labour in Guyana, Mrs. Locke's own description of her work is of interest:

This mural illustrates in general terms the development of the labour movement in Guyana, from the days of slavery to the present time.

In the beginning one sees the plantation owner dominating the slaves by force. It is they who worked in his house and on the plantation, clearing the land, digging the drainage canals and reaping the crops of sugar and cotton. Child labour is represented by the boy leading a heavily laden donkey. Immediately above the donkey is a scene taken from a contemporary painting of the passing of the Emancipation Bill at the public building. A slave owner is riding in his horse and carriage, driven by his house slaves. Further along are two women hoeing a plot of sugar cane. They are followed by the arrival of indentured immigrant sugar workers.

The colour in the mural is sombre to begin with, gradually brightening as the workers successfully educate for better conditions. Still the white overseer is there to give orders and to direct. The people are able to own land and plant crops, such as rice, and are raised from the level of total manual labour to greater skills with the start of the use of machinery on the land and in industry.

Next, there is an area in the mural where dock workers load bags of sugar, followed by two men marching with placards, symbolizing the beginning of the trade union movement.

Finally, the present day labour situation is seen as being one where the individual worker is at last receiving fair treatment with improved working facilities and opportunities for both men and women.

Early in 1969 the ILO advised me that they wanted me to assume my new responsibilities in Asia as soon as possible. I realized that I had already been in Guyana for 16 months, well beyond the original assignment of one year. Yet I felt I should be allowed to remain until at least most of the project was completed, which I estimated to be shortly after May Day.

We then planned to have the traditional May Day-Labour Day parade terminate on the College grounds, followed by opening ceremonies in the college auditorium. My wife, Anne, and I joined several thousand workers in the long march to the College. The workers were not exactly marching with the precision of a military parade: they were a laughing, happy, banner-carrying crowd on their way to their own new labour centre.

The opening ceremonies took place in the evening. While the auditorium was designed to accommodate only 350, there was a crowd of some 750 packed into the auditorium and the adjoining courtyard.

Charles Holmes, the resident representative of the United Nations Development Programme (UNDP), described the scene in his official report:

> After the sessions were over, everyone was invited to walk around the building, and drinks were served from the College cafeteria. Among the centres of attraction was the lounge, a very handsome room walled with Guyanese wood, which the Board of Governors of the College announced had been named "The Swerdlow Room."

Greetings were received from a number of unions outside Guyana, and from other sources, including Paul Hoffman, administrator of the United Nations Development Programme. His message was particularly significant because he rarely sent messages on such occasions. After extending greetings to all involved in the College, he continued:

> Critchlow Labour College is unique, or very nearly so, in the developing world. It is proper that it should now be able to live in a handsome and functional home, of which any country would be proud.
>
> I should like to send friendly greetings to our brother organization, the ILO, whose association and appointment of Mr. Max Swerdlow has done so much to make today's celebration possible.
>
> Although the United Nations Development Programme has not participated in the creation of Critchlow Labour College, I do not speak from the sidelines. The UNDP is heavily engaged with the ILO as the executing agency in over $300,000,000 (U.S.) worth of projects of the advancement of labour in the developing world.
>
> The dedication of Critchlow Labour College will surely be among the most important events of this year of the celebration of the 50th anniversary of the ILO.
>
> The Government of Guyana, the TUC, and the private firms and individuals of this country may well be proud of having stretched so high to set a mark for others to attempt to reach.

Prime Minister Forbes Burnham gave the main address and declared the building open. For me, the ceremony was deeply emotional, and a never-to-be-forgotten experience. When the Chairman of the Board of Governors announced that the common room was to be designated as "The Swerdlow Room," tears welled in my eyes. The event was the realization of a dream that had not even been a dream the year before. Yet, I did not regard all this as a personal triumph. I doubt very much if the same could have been accomplished in so short a time in any other country. The success of my mission was due to the nation-wide spirit of self-help and co-operation that prevailed in Guyana at that time. I had enjoyed working with the people, transcending geographic boundaries. Together we had broadened horizons, opened new vistas, and created opportunities which would enrich the lives of workers for years to come.

The *Guyana Graphic* in a lead editorial, described the event held on May Day as "most significant and appropriate." Referring to the College being named after one of the country's great labour leaders, the editorial continued:

It is consistent with Critchlow's belief in compromise that a Canadian, in the person of Mr. Max Swerdlow, has done so much to make the construction of the college an accomplished fact. Mr. Swerdlow, who arrived in Guyana in 1957, has shown a dedication to the College in particular and labour in general, which is exemplary in a developing nation such as Guyana, where such virtues are among the qualities which are most relevant in developing national conduct.

On our way to the airport, we had the taxi driver go by way of the College, and there we stopped for a moment, seeing the reality of the dream we had shared. Leaving Guyana was an emotional experience. Once we were airborne I could hardly wait for the hostess to serve drinks. I took two double gin and tonics and then reclined, slowly, ever so slowly, beginning to relax. Anne, who understood my mood, was silent.

My thoughts drifted in many directions: the anxiety about my new assignment in Asia, the uncertainty of my continued employment, the difficulties, joys, and indeed the privilege of having participated in building the Critchlow Labour College.

As we moved further and further from Guyana my thoughts drifted from the College. It was not unusual for me to quickly become emotionally detached from a completed project and become preoccupied with the new involvement. I took my new "Terms of Reference" from my briefcase and, for the first time since I had received them, I began to seriously examine my responsibilities in the vast region of my Asian assignment.

My official title was "ILO Regional Advisor on Workers' Education in Asia." My responsibilities, in broad general terms, were "to assist trade unions in Asian countries to initiate and develop workers' education activities." The region consisted of 21 countries.

But, as I read the terms of reference, I had no idea and could not possibly visualize the immensity and the profound diversity of that region. It was only after working there for several years that I began to better understand the complexities of the area. I remained in Asia for more than seven years, and when I left in 1975, I wrote in part:

Asia is half of humanity. The Region (ILO) encompasses twenty-one countries of marked contrast. Some are developed democracies, others are governed by martial law. Some live in peace, others are at war. Some countries are amongst the richest in the world, others are poorest. Millions live in large modern cities and work in highly mechanized industries, and many more millions live in isolated villages on subsistence agriculture. In these small communities customs, values, attitudes based on centuries of cultural and sociological traditions, are deep rooted. To such people, the progress of the 20th century is often obscure and irrelevant. Many are with hope and determination for a better and more meaningful life, and many others without hope live in the shadows of the past.

Although I knew very little about Asia in the beginning, I realized that working there would not be the same as it had been in the Caribbean. I anticipated some difficulties, disappointments and frustrations. Nevertheless, I really believed, and indeed was committed to making a worthy contribution to workers' education and the labour movement in Asia. I accepted the assignment with deep enthusiasm and a sense of adventure of great magnitude.

Those were my thoughts on the flight from Guyana to Canada in May 1969. Then, for some strange reason, I recalled my last ride in a box car on May Day 1934. Those thirty-five elapsed years seemed a long, long time ago.

Postscript
The Future of Trade Unions in Canada

WILL TRADE UNIONS IN CANADA be the same in 2015 as they are today in 1990? Generally speaking, "I'd say yes," they will continue to counterbalance the power and influence of industry, they will continue to strive for the economic improvement of their members, and generally they will push for better conditions of life and work. How well unions will succeed will depend on how relevant they become to the significant changes taking place both in industry and in the country.

The social climate in which unions function has a great bearing on their broader social involvement. Unions should not only be regarded as legal entities as they are too often today. They must also be accepted as socially desirable institutions, essential pre-requisites for democracy. Given the necessary climate for growth and development the horizons and responsibilities of the trade union movement of the future will be much wider and broader then those of today. Collective bargaining may well remain the core concern of trade unions, but in addition the total social welfare of the working people of Canada will be added to their agenda. This total social concern will encompass every facet of workers lives.

The labour movement must demonstrate as much concern about the state of the planet as it does about shorter hours or higher wages.

The labour movement must express as much concern about the total health of Canadian citizens as it does about trade union rights and responsibilities.

I believe that the labour movement of the future will not be able to choose one priority against another. Indeed I think the current dichotomy between total social welfare and narrow trade union concerns will disappear.

The labour leader of the future will be a person who has the broadest view of social development and of social concerns. To further such social concerns political involvement will be a critical necessity. While collective bargaining may achieve some gains, most must be gained in the political arena.

I cannot predict whether there will be more or fewer strikes or larger or smaller unions, but I can predict that tomorrow's labour leader must be concerned with the Gross National Happiness not just the Gross National Product. I can also predict that as long as exploitation exists, the labour movement will be the vehicle of people's struggle to overcome it.